METASPLOIT

MASTERCLASS FOR ETHICAL HACKERS

EXPERT PENETRATION TESTING AND VULNERABILITY ASSESSMENT

4 BOOKS IN 1

BOOK 1
METASPLOIT MASTERCLASS: NETWORK RECONNAISSANCE AND
VULNERABILITY SCANNING

BOOK 2
METASPLOIT MASTERCLASS: WEB APPLICATION PENETRATION TESTING

BOOK 3
METASPLOIT MASTERCLASS: WIRELESS AND IOT HACKING

BOOK 4
METASPLOIT MASTERCLASS: ADVANCED THREAT DETECTION AND
DEFENSE

ROB BOTWRIGHT

Published by Rob Botwright
Library of Congress Cataloging-in-Publication Data
ISBN 978-1-83938-570-4
Cover design by Rizzo

Disclaimer

The contents of this book are based on extensive research and the best available historical sources. However, the author and publisher make no claims, promises, or guarantees about the accuracy, completeness, or adequacy of the information contained herein. The information in this book is provided on an "as is" basis, and the author and publisher disclaim any and all liability for any errors, omissions, or inaccuracies in the information or for any actions taken in reliance on such information. The opinions and views expressed in this book are those of the author and do not necessarily reflect the official policy or position of any organization or individual mentioned in this book. Any reference to specific people, places, or events is intended only to provide historical context and is not intended to defame or malign any group, individual, or entity. The information in this book is intended for educational and entertainment purposes only. It is not intended to be a substitute for professional advice or judgment. Readers are encouraged to conduct their own research and to seek professional advice where appropriate. Every effort has been made to obtain necessary permissions and acknowledgments for all images and other copyrighted material used in this book. Any errors or omissions in this regard are unintentional, and the author and publisher will correct them in future editions.

TABLE OF CONTENTS – BOOK 1 - METASPLOIT MASTERCLASS: NETWORK RECONNAISSANCE AND VULNERABILITY SCANNING

TABLE OF CONTENTS – BOOK 2 - METASPLOIT MASTERCLASS: WEB APPLICATION PENETRATION TESTING

TABLE OF CONTENTS – BOOK 3 - METASPLOIT MASTERCLASS: WIRELESS AND IOT HACKING

TABLE OF CONTENTS – BOOK 4 - METASPLOIT MASTERCLASS: ADVANCED THREAT DETECTION AND DEFENSE

Introduction

Welcome to the "Metasploit Masterclass for Ethical Hackers" book bundle, a comprehensive and all-encompassing exploration of the exciting and ever-evolving world of ethical hacking, penetration testing, and vulnerability assessment. In a digital landscape where threats loom large and security is paramount, this bundle equips you with the knowledge, tools, and techniques to become a proficient ethical hacker and a formidable defender of cyberspace.

In today's interconnected world, the importance of cybersecurity cannot be overstated. With cyberattacks becoming increasingly sophisticated and widespread, the need for skilled professionals who can protect systems, networks, and data has never been greater. This book bundle, comprising four expertly crafted volumes, is designed to meet that need head-on.

Book 1: Metasploit Masterclass: Network Reconnaissance and Vulnerability Scanning In this first volume, you'll embark on a journey into the fundamentals of ethical hacking. Network reconnaissance and vulnerability scanning are the cornerstones of cybersecurity, and here you'll learn how to master them. You'll discover how to gather critical information about target networks, identify potential vulnerabilities, and perform comprehensive vulnerability scanning. By the end of this book, you'll have laid a solid foundation upon which to build your ethical hacking skills.

Book 2: Metasploit Masterclass: Web Application Penetration Testing The second volume delves into the intricate realm of web application security. Web applications are the lifeblood of the digital world, and they are prime targets for cybercriminals. This book provides you with the knowledge and expertise needed to identify, exploit, and secure vulnerabilities in web applications. You'll gain hands-on experience in assessing web application security, making you an invaluable asset in protecting the online assets of organizations.

Book 3: Metasploit Masterclass: Wireless and IoT Hacking With the proliferation of wireless networks and IoT devices, new attack vectors and vulnerabilities emerge daily. Book 3 unveils the world of wireless and IoT hacking, teaching you how to exploit these technologies and gain unauthorized access. By understanding the vulnerabilities in wireless networks and IoT devices, you'll be better equipped to secure them effectively.

Book 4: Metasploit Masterclass: Advanced Threat Detection and Defense The final volume of this bundle takes you to the cutting edge of cybersecurity. Here, you'll explore advanced threat detection methods, proactive threat hunting, and the use of Metasploit for defensive purposes. Armed with this knowledge, you'll be prepared to defend against even the most sophisticated cyber threats.

As you journey through these four books, you'll not only learn the techniques of ethical hacking but also the principles of cybersecurity, the importance of responsible and legal hacking, and the critical role of ethical hackers in safeguarding digital assets. Whether you're a newcomer looking to embark on an exciting career in cybersecurity or an experienced professional seeking to enhance your skills, this bundle offers a holistic and hands-on approach to mastering the art and science of ethical hacking.

So, prepare to dive deep into the world of ethical hacking, armed with the Metasploit framework, a versatile and powerful tool in the hands of those who wield it responsibly. Let this "Metasploit Masterclass for Ethical Hackers" book bundle be your guide and companion on your journey to becoming an ethical hacking expert and a guardian of the digital realm.

BOOK 1
METASPLOIT MASTERCLASS
NETWORK RECONNAISSANCE AND VULNERABILITY SCANNING

ROB BOTWRIGHT

Chapter 1: Introduction to Network Reconnaissance

In this chapter, we'll delve into the fascinating world of network reconnaissance, a critical phase in the realm of ethical hacking and penetration testing. Network reconnaissance serves as the initial step of gathering information about a target network or system, providing valuable insights that will shape the course of your assessment. It's like being a detective, piecing together clues to understand the target's infrastructure and potential vulnerabilities. Network reconnaissance is all about information gathering, which includes understanding the target's IP addresses, subnets, and domain names. This information serves as your foundation for future penetration testing activities, enabling you to identify potential entry points into the target network. By comprehensively scanning and mapping the network, you'll gain a clearer picture of its architecture and potential security weaknesses.

One of the primary goals of network reconnaissance is to identify active hosts within the target network, as these are the systems you'll be examining closely for vulnerabilities and potential exploits. You'll use a variety of tools and techniques to achieve this, from basic network scanning to more advanced methods. Additionally, network reconnaissance involves analyzing the network's structure to uncover the relationships between different systems, services, and devices. This insight will help you make informed decisions about your penetration testing approach and prioritize your efforts effectively.

When it comes to network reconnaissance, you need to consider both passive and active techniques. Passive reconnaissance involves gathering information without directly interacting with the target network. This can include examining publicly available information, such as DNS records, WHOIS data, and social media profiles associated with the organization. Passive reconnaissance is a crucial first step, allowing you to understand the target's digital footprint and potential weak points.

Active reconnaissance, on the other hand, involves direct interaction with the target network to collect information actively. This may include techniques like network scanning, banner grabbing, and OS fingerprinting. Active reconnaissance is more intrusive and can potentially be detected by intrusion detection systems (IDS) or other security measures. Therefore, it's essential to approach it carefully, keeping stealth and evasion in mind.

Understanding the difference between these two reconnaissance approaches is fundamental to a successful penetration test. You'll often combine passive and active reconnaissance to build a comprehensive profile of the target. Passive reconnaissance provides a starting point, while active reconnaissance helps validate and expand the information you've gathered.

As you embark on your journey of network reconnaissance, you'll become familiar with various tools and utilities designed to aid you in this phase. These tools range from basic command-line utilities like ping, traceroute, and nslookup to more specialized tools such as Nmap, Wireshark, and Shodan. Each of these tools serves a unique purpose, helping you gather specific types of information about the target network.

Nmap, for example, is a versatile and widely used network scanning tool that can discover open ports, identify services running on those ports, and even determine the operating system of the target system. It's an essential tool in your reconnaissance toolkit. Similarly, Wireshark allows you to capture and analyze network traffic, providing valuable insights into the communication patterns and potential vulnerabilities within the network.

Beyond tools, you'll also explore techniques like banner grabbing, which involves connecting to open ports on a target system to retrieve information about the services running on those ports. This can reveal version numbers and other details that help you identify potential vulnerabilities.

In addition to passive and active reconnaissance, you'll learn about the importance of information sources such as WHOIS databases, DNS records, and search engines. These sources can provide critical information about the target organization, including domain names, IP addresses, and contact information. Leveraging these sources effectively can save you time and help you build a more comprehensive reconnaissance profile.

It's essential to note that network reconnaissance is not a one-size-fits-all process. The techniques and tools you use will vary depending on the target's size, complexity, and the specific goals of your penetration test. For example, a small business network may have a simpler infrastructure compared to a large enterprise network with multiple branches and data centers. Your reconnaissance approach must adapt accordingly.

As you progress through this chapter, you'll gain practical experience in conducting network reconnaissance, using real-world examples and scenarios. You'll learn how to leverage various tools and techniques to gather critical information, identify potential vulnerabilities, and lay the groundwork for the subsequent phases of penetration testing. Network reconnaissance is the foundation upon which the rest of your ethical hacking journey is built, and mastering it is essential to becoming a skilled penetration tester.

Next, we'll delve deeper into the objectives and scope of reconnaissance, understanding the essential aspects that guide this critical phase of ethical hacking and penetration testing. Network reconnaissance serves as the initial step of gathering information about a target network or system, providing valuable insights that shape the course of your assessment. Think of it as the foundation upon which the rest of your ethical hacking journey is built. The primary goal of reconnaissance is to gain a comprehensive understanding of the target environment, its infrastructure, and potential vulnerabilities.

Reconnaissance involves a systematic approach to information gathering, and it's not a one-size-fits-all process. The specific objectives of your reconnaissance efforts may vary depending on the nature of the engagement and your goals. Whether you're conducting a penetration test for a client or evaluating your organization's security posture, reconnaissance helps you gather the necessary intelligence to make informed decisions.

One of the fundamental objectives of reconnaissance is to identify active hosts within the target network. These are the systems that are currently online and accessible.

Identifying active hosts is crucial because they are the primary focus of your penetration testing activities. These hosts represent potential entry points into the target network, and understanding them is essential for a successful assessment.

Reconnaissance also aims to map the target network's architecture and understand how different systems and devices are interconnected. This mapping process helps you identify potential weaknesses and vulnerabilities in the network's design. It allows you to see the bigger picture and determine how different elements of the network interact with each other.

Another key objective of reconnaissance is to gather information about the target's IP addresses, subnets, and domain names. This information provides a starting point for your assessment, helping you narrow down the scope of your activities and target specific areas of interest. It's like having a map that guides you through the vast landscape of the target network.

In addition to identifying hosts and mapping the network, reconnaissance aims to uncover information about the target's services and applications. This includes details about open ports, running services, and their versions. Knowing which services are in use and their versions is critical for identifying potential vulnerabilities that can be exploited during the penetration testing phase.

Reconnaissance also extends to understanding the organization's external-facing infrastructure, including its web applications, email servers, and public-facing services. This external view is essential for assessing the organization's attack surface, as it helps you identify potential entry points from the internet.

The scope of reconnaissance goes beyond just technical aspects. It also includes gathering information about the organization itself. This can involve researching the organization's employees, social media presence, and any publicly available information about the company's history and operations. Understanding the organization's culture and potential weak points can be valuable during the later phases of penetration testing.

It's important to emphasize that reconnaissance should always be conducted within the boundaries of legality and ethical guidelines. You should obtain proper authorization and consent before conducting any reconnaissance activities, especially when performing penetration tests for clients. Respecting privacy and adhering to legal regulations is a fundamental aspect of ethical hacking.

As you embark on your reconnaissance journey, you'll become familiar with various tools and techniques designed to aid you in this phase. These tools range from basic command-line utilities like ping, traceroute, and nslookup to more specialized tools such as Nmap, Wireshark, and Shodan. Each of these tools serves a unique purpose, helping you gather specific types of information about the target network.

Nmap, for example, is a versatile network scanning tool that can discover open ports, identify services running on those ports, and even determine the operating system of the target system. It's an essential tool in your reconnaissance toolkit. Similarly, Wireshark allows you to capture and analyze network traffic, providing valuable insights into communication patterns and potential vulnerabilities within the network.

Beyond tools, reconnaissance also involves leveraging information sources such as WHOIS databases, DNS records, and search engines. These sources can provide critical information about the target organization, including domain names, IP addresses, and contact information. Effective use of these sources can save you time and help you build a more comprehensive reconnaissance profile.

Throughout your reconnaissance activities, it's essential to maintain a well-documented record of the information you gather. Proper documentation ensures that you have a clear record of your findings, which is crucial for reporting and decision-making in later phases of the penetration test. Your documentation should include details about discovered hosts, services, vulnerabilities, and any relevant contextual information.

In summary, the objectives and scope of reconnaissance are vast and multifaceted. It's a process that combines technical expertise, research skills, and a thorough understanding of the target environment. As you delve deeper into this phase, you'll discover the art of information gathering and its pivotal role in the ethical hacking and penetration testing journey. It's the stage where you lay the groundwork for the exciting challenges that lie ahead in the world of cybersecurity.

Chapter 2: Scanning and Enumeration Techniques

Scanning plays a crucial role in the realm of penetration testing, and it's an integral part of the reconnaissance phase. It's akin to shining a spotlight on the target network, revealing potential vulnerabilities and entry points for further exploration. Scanning involves actively probing the target's systems and services to gather more detailed information than passive reconnaissance methods can provide.

The primary objective of scanning is to identify open ports on target systems. Ports act as communication endpoints, allowing various services and applications to interact with the network. An open port means that a service or application is actively listening for incoming connections, and this information is valuable to a penetration tester.

Understanding which ports are open can help you determine the services running on a system. Each service is associated with a specific port number, and identifying these services is a critical step in assessing potential vulnerabilities. By knowing which services are in use, you can research known vulnerabilities associated with those services and plan your attack accordingly.

Scanning also helps in mapping the network topology, revealing how systems are interconnected and which devices are directly accessible from the internet. This network map provides a visual representation of the target environment and is essential for planning your penetration testing activities.

There are several scanning techniques and tools available to penetration testers. The choice of technique and tool

depends on the goals of the assessment and the information you seek. One of the most commonly used scanning tools is Nmap (Network Mapper). Nmap is a versatile and powerful tool that can perform a wide range of network scans.

With Nmap, you can conduct a basic TCP connect scan to identify open ports and services. You can also perform a more stealthy SYN scan, which sends SYN packets to the target ports without establishing a full connection. This method is less likely to trigger intrusion detection systems. Beyond port scanning, Nmap can also perform service version detection. This means that it can determine the specific version of a service running on an open port. Knowing the service version is crucial because different versions of the same service may have different vulnerabilities.

Another valuable feature of Nmap is its ability to perform OS fingerprinting. By analyzing the responses to certain probes, Nmap can make educated guesses about the target's operating system. This information is useful for tailoring your attack methods to the target environment accurately.

In addition to Nmap, there are other scanning tools like Masscan, Zmap, and Nessus, each with its unique capabilities and use cases. Masscan, for instance, is known for its speed and is suitable for quickly scanning large networks. Nessus, on the other hand, is a vulnerability scanner that can not only identify open ports but also assess the vulnerabilities associated with those ports.

Scanning should always be conducted methodically and with careful consideration of the potential impact on the target network. The goal is to gather information without causing disruption or triggering security alarms. Techniques such as SYN scans and idle scans are designed to be less intrusive and are often preferred in penetration testing engagements.

While scanning is an essential step in the penetration testing process, it's vital to conduct it responsibly and ethically. Unauthorized scanning of systems and networks can lead to legal and ethical issues. Always obtain proper authorization before conducting any scanning activities, especially when working on behalf of a client.

In summary, scanning is a critical phase in penetration testing, serving as a bridge between reconnaissance and exploitation. It allows you to identify open ports, discover services and their versions, and map the network topology. With the right scanning techniques and tools, you can gather the information needed to plan your attack strategies effectively. However, responsible and ethical scanning practices are paramount to ensure a successful and legally compliant penetration testing engagement.

Now that we've explored the significance of scanning in penetration testing, it's time to delve deeper into the next crucial phase: enumeration. Enumeration is the process of extracting detailed information about the target systems and services identified during scanning. It's like opening the doors and peering inside to gather insights into what's happening within the target network.

Enumeration plays a pivotal role in the reconnaissance phase because it provides a more comprehensive view of the target's infrastructure. While scanning helps identify open ports and services, enumeration goes a step further by extracting valuable details about those services. This includes user accounts, shares, software versions, and more.

The primary goal of enumeration is to discover as much information as possible about the target systems, with the aim of identifying potential vulnerabilities and weaknesses. Enumeration helps you uncover hidden gems of information that might not be readily visible during scanning but can be critical for your penetration testing efforts.

Enumeration methods can vary depending on the target's operating system, services, and network configuration. One common method involves querying the Domain Name System (DNS) for hostnames, IP addresses, and other domain-related information. DNS enumeration can reveal essential details about the target's internal network structure and naming conventions.

Another critical enumeration technique involves querying the Lightweight Directory Access Protocol (LDAP) service. LDAP enumeration is particularly useful when assessing Windows-based networks. It can provide a wealth of information, such as user accounts, groups, organizational units, and more. This information is invaluable for identifying potential targets and entry points.

Additionally, Network Time Protocol (NTP) enumeration can be utilized to gather information about the target's time synchronization settings and potentially identify vulnerable systems. NTP enumeration can reveal servers running outdated or vulnerable versions of the NTP service.

While manual enumeration techniques are effective, there are also specialized tools available to streamline the process. One widely used tool for Windows enumeration is enum4linux, which extracts user and group information from Windows machines. Enum4linux can be a valuable asset in a penetration tester's toolkit when assessing Windows-based environments.

For Linux systems, the enum4linux counterpart is enum4linux-ng, which focuses on gathering information from Linux-based SMB services. These tools automate the process of querying SMB (Server Message Block) shares for information like usernames, shares, and more.

Another notable enumeration tool is SNMP enumeration software, which leverages the Simple Network Management Protocol (SNMP) to gather data about network devices, including routers, switches, and printers. SNMP enumeration can provide insights into network architecture and device configurations.

When assessing web applications, web enumeration tools like DirBuster or Gobuster can be invaluable. These tools are designed to identify hidden directories and files within web applications. They work by making a series of HTTP requests, checking for common directory and file names that may not be explicitly linked in the application's web pages.

Enumeration isn't limited to querying specific services or protocols. It can also involve brute-force attacks to guess credentials for services like SSH, FTP, or Telnet. These attacks involve trying a multitude of username and password combinations until a valid one is found. While effective, brute-force attacks should be approached with caution, as they can lock out accounts or trigger security alerts.

In addition to the methods and tools mentioned above, there are countless other enumeration techniques and tools available to penetration testers, each suited to different scenarios and target environments. The key to successful enumeration lies in understanding the target's infrastructure, identifying potential information sources, and selecting the most appropriate methods and tools for the task.

However, it's essential to approach enumeration responsibly and ethically. Unauthorized enumeration can disrupt network operations, trigger security alarms, or even result in legal consequences. Always obtain proper authorization and adhere to ethical guidelines when conducting enumeration activities during penetration testing engagements.

In summary, enumeration is a critical phase in penetration testing that involves extracting detailed information about target systems and services. It helps uncover hidden vulnerabilities and weaknesses within the target infrastructure, providing valuable insights for penetration testers. Enumeration methods and tools vary based on the target's environment, but they all share the goal of gaining a deeper understanding of the target's inner workings. Responsible and ethical enumeration practices are essential to ensure a successful and legally compliant penetration testing engagement.

Chapter 3: Vulnerability Assessment Fundamentals

As we progress in our journey through penetration testing, it's essential to delve into the fundamentals of vulnerability assessment, a critical aspect of understanding and mitigating security risks. Vulnerability assessment serves as a vital component of the overall cybersecurity strategy, allowing organizations to identify, evaluate, and prioritize potential weaknesses within their systems, applications, and network infrastructure.

At its core, vulnerability assessment is the systematic process of discovering, classifying, and assessing vulnerabilities within an organization's assets. These vulnerabilities can range from software flaws and misconfigurations to weak security practices or outdated systems. The primary goal of vulnerability assessment is to provide organizations with a clear understanding of their security posture and the potential risks they face.

One of the key aspects of vulnerability assessment is asset discovery. Before you can assess vulnerabilities, you need to know what assets are present within the organization's environment. This includes identifying servers, workstations, network devices, applications, and databases. Comprehensive asset discovery is crucial because it ensures that no critical components are overlooked during the assessment.

Once assets are identified, the next step is vulnerability scanning. Vulnerability scanning involves using automated tools to scan the network and systems for known vulnerabilities. These tools compare the configuration and software versions of assets against a database of known vulnerabilities to identify potential weaknesses. Vulnerability scanning helps organizations pinpoint areas that require immediate attention and remediation.

Vulnerability assessment doesn't stop at automated scanning; it also encompasses manual testing and analysis. This includes in-depth examination of system configurations, security policies, and practices to identify vulnerabilities that may not be detectable through automated means. Manual testing allows for a more thorough evaluation of the organization's security posture.

The output of a vulnerability assessment typically includes a list of identified vulnerabilities, along with their severity ratings and potential impacts. Vulnerabilities are often categorized based on their severity, ranging from low-risk issues to critical vulnerabilities that require immediate attention. This categorization helps organizations prioritize remediation efforts based on the potential impact on their security.

Beyond identifying vulnerabilities, vulnerability assessment also plays a crucial role in risk management. Organizations must assess the potential risks associated with each vulnerability to make informed decisions about mitigation. This involves considering factors such as the likelihood of exploitation, the impact on business operations, and the cost of remediation.

To effectively manage risk, organizations may choose to accept, mitigate, transfer, or avoid vulnerabilities. Mitigation strategies may include applying patches, configuring security settings, or implementing compensating controls to reduce the risk associated with a vulnerability. Vulnerability assessment helps organizations make these risk-based decisions and allocate resources accordingly.

Vulnerability assessment tools and solutions vary in complexity and capabilities. Some tools are designed for continuous monitoring and real-time vulnerability assessment, while others are used for periodic assessments. Organizations should choose tools that align with their specific needs and objectives.

Common vulnerability assessment tools include Nessus, Qualys, OpenVAS, and Rapid7's Nexpose, among others. These tools offer a wide range of features, including asset discovery, vulnerability scanning, reporting, and integration with other security solutions. The choice of tool often depends on factors like the organization's size, budget, and existing infrastructure.

While vulnerability assessment is a crucial component of cybersecurity, it's important to note that it's not a one-time activity. Security risks evolve over time, and new vulnerabilities are discovered regularly. Therefore, organizations should establish a continuous vulnerability assessment program to stay vigilant and adapt to emerging threats.

Moreover, vulnerability assessment is closely tied to the broader concept of vulnerability management. Vulnerability management encompasses the entire lifecycle of vulnerabilities, including identification, assessment, remediation, and validation. It's a proactive approach to addressing vulnerabilities that extends beyond assessment to ensure that identified weaknesses are effectively resolved.

Ethical hackers and penetration testers play a significant role in the vulnerability assessment process. They leverage their expertise to identify and assess vulnerabilities from an attacker's perspective. This helps organizations understand not only what vulnerabilities exist but also how they could be exploited by malicious actors.

In summary, the fundamentals of vulnerability assessment are essential for organizations seeking to strengthen their security posture. This process involves asset discovery, automated scanning, manual testing, risk assessment, and mitigation planning. Vulnerability assessment tools and solutions are instrumental in this endeavor, helping organizations identify weaknesses and make informed decisions to protect their assets and data. It's an ongoing effort that requires continuous monitoring and adaptation to stay ahead of evolving threats in the dynamic landscape of cybersecurity. Now that we've delved into the fundamentals of vulnerability assessment, it's time to explore the various approaches to vulnerability scanning. Vulnerability scanning is a critical element of the assessment process, as it allows organizations to proactively identify and assess potential weaknesses within their systems and networks.

One common approach to vulnerability scanning is agent-based scanning. In this method, a small software agent is installed on each target system, enabling it to communicate directly with the vulnerability scanning tool. This approach provides detailed insights into the vulnerabilities and configurations of individual systems, making it ideal for environments with diverse operating systems and configurations.

Agentless scanning, on the other hand, does not require the installation of software agents on target systems. Instead, it relies on network-based scanning techniques to identify vulnerabilities. This approach is less intrusive and more suitable for scenarios where installing agents is impractical or not allowed.

Another distinction in vulnerability scanning approaches is active scanning versus passive scanning. Active scanning involves sending requests to target systems to assess their vulnerabilities actively. This method is more thorough but can potentially impact the performance of the target systems and may trigger security alerts.

Passive scanning, on the other hand, observes network traffic and collects information without actively engaging with target systems. It's less intrusive and typically goes unnoticed by the systems being assessed. Passive scanning is useful for continuous monitoring and can provide insights into vulnerabilities as they emerge.

Authenticated scanning is yet another approach that involves scanning systems with valid credentials, such as usernames and passwords. This approach offers a higher level of access and provides a more accurate assessment of vulnerabilities, as it can examine system configurations and settings that may not be accessible during unauthenticated scans.

However, authenticated scanning requires careful management of credentials and raises security considerations, as compromising the scanning credentials could lead to unauthorized access. It's crucial to implement secure practices when conducting authenticated scans to protect sensitive information.

Furthermore, vulnerability scanning can be categorized as credentialed scanning or non-credentialed scanning. In credentialed scanning, the scanning tool has the necessary credentials to access and authenticate with the target systems fully. This allows for a more comprehensive assessment of vulnerabilities, including configuration issues.

Non-credentialed scanning, on the other hand, does not rely on credentials and assesses vulnerabilities from an external perspective, similar to how an attacker would approach the system. While non-credentialed scanning provides valuable insights, it may miss certain vulnerabilities related to system configurations that require authentication for assessment.

Scheduled scanning versus continuous scanning is another distinction to consider. Scheduled scanning is conducted at predefined intervals, such as weekly or monthly. This approach provides periodic snapshots of the organization's security posture and allows for proactive vulnerability management. Continuous scanning, on the other hand, is an ongoing process that monitors systems and networks in real-time. It provides immediate visibility into newly discovered vulnerabilities and allows organizations to respond rapidly to emerging threats. Continuous scanning is particularly valuable in dynamic environments where changes occur frequently.

Cloud-based vulnerability scanning is becoming increasingly relevant as organizations migrate their infrastructure to the cloud. In this approach, vulnerability scanning tools are hosted in the cloud and scan cloud-based resources and services. This provides flexibility and scalability, especially for organizations with hybrid or multi-cloud environments.

Moreover, vulnerability scanning can be categorized based on its focus. External scanning assesses vulnerabilities from an external perspective, simulating how an attacker would approach the organization from the internet. It helps identify weaknesses that could be exploited by external threats.

Internal scanning, on the other hand, assesses vulnerabilities from within the organization's network. It examines systems and services that are accessible only from within the network, helping identify potential insider threats and vulnerabilities that may not be visible externally.

Integrated scanning solutions combine multiple scanning approaches and techniques to provide a holistic view of an organization's security posture. These solutions offer flexibility in tailoring scanning activities to specific needs and environments.

It's essential to choose the vulnerability scanning approach that aligns with your organization's goals, resources, and risk tolerance. The choice may depend on factors such as the organization's size, complexity, compliance requirements, and the nature of the systems and networks being assessed. Regardless of the approach chosen, it's crucial to conduct vulnerability scanning as part of a comprehensive vulnerability management program. This includes not only identifying vulnerabilities but also prioritizing them based on their severity, potential impact, and likelihood of exploitation.

Vulnerability scanning is a proactive measure to strengthen an organization's security posture, providing valuable insights into potential weaknesses before they can be exploited by malicious actors. It's an essential component of a robust cybersecurity strategy in today's dynamic threat landscape.

Chapter 4: Metasploit Framework Essentials

Let's dive into the exciting world of the Metasploit Framework, a powerful and versatile penetration testing tool that has become a cornerstone of ethical hacking and cybersecurity. Metasploit is like a Swiss Army knife for security professionals, offering a wide range of capabilities to assess and secure computer systems and networks.

At its core, the Metasploit Framework is an open-source penetration testing platform that enables security experts to identify and exploit vulnerabilities in target systems. It's a valuable tool for both offensive and defensive purposes, making it an essential asset in the toolkit of ethical hackers, penetration testers, and security professionals.

Metasploit simplifies the process of testing and assessing the security of systems and applications. It provides a structured and organized framework for conducting penetration tests, helping testers effectively identify, exploit, and remediate vulnerabilities. This structured approach makes it easier to discover weaknesses and assess potential risks.

One of the standout features of the Metasploit Framework is its extensive database of known vulnerabilities and exploits. The Metasploit database includes a vast repository of exploits, payloads, and auxiliary modules that can be used to simulate attacks and assess the security of target systems. This database is continually updated, ensuring that testers have access to the latest exploit techniques and payloads.

Metasploit's modular architecture is another key advantage. It's designed to be highly modular, allowing users to customize and extend its functionality easily. The framework consists of different modules, each serving a specific purpose. These modules can be combined and customized to create tailored attack scenarios.

The three primary module types in Metasploit are exploits, payloads, and auxiliary modules. Exploits are used to take advantage of vulnerabilities in target systems. Payloads are code snippets that run on exploited systems, allowing testers to control and manipulate them. Auxiliary modules provide additional functionality, such as scanning, fingerprinting, and brute-force attacks.

Metasploit's ease of use is a significant benefit, especially for security professionals who may not have extensive programming or scripting skills. It provides a user-friendly command-line interface and a graphical user interface (GUI) called Armitage, making it accessible to users of varying skill levels.

The Metasploit Framework supports multiple operating systems and platforms, ensuring compatibility with a wide range of target systems. It allows testers to assess the security of Windows, Linux, macOS, and various network devices, making it versatile for testing diverse environments.

Metasploit also offers a collaborative and community-driven ecosystem. Users can share their own exploits, modules, and payloads with the community, contributing to the framework's growth and effectiveness. This collaborative aspect fosters innovation and ensures that Metasploit remains a cutting-edge tool in the field of cybersecurity.

While Metasploit is a powerful offensive tool, it can also be used for defensive purposes. Security professionals and organizations can leverage Metasploit to assess and improve their own security measures. By simulating attacks and identifying vulnerabilities, they can proactively strengthen their defenses and reduce the risk of real-world breaches.

Furthermore, Metasploit's reporting capabilities are essential for documenting and communicating findings. It generates detailed reports that can be used to convey the results of penetration tests to stakeholders, management, and IT teams. These reports provide a clear picture of vulnerabilities, risks, and recommended remediation steps.

Metasploit is continually evolving to meet the changing demands of the cybersecurity landscape. Rapid7, the company behind Metasploit, actively maintains and updates the framework to address emerging threats and vulnerabilities. This commitment to development and security ensures that Metasploit remains a reliable tool for security professionals.

In summary, the Metasploit Framework is a versatile and indispensable tool in the field of ethical hacking and cybersecurity. It provides a structured and modular approach to penetration testing, simplifying the process of identifying and exploiting vulnerabilities. With its extensive database of exploits, payloads, and auxiliary modules, Metasploit empowers testers to assess the security of a wide range of systems and platforms.

Metasploit's ease of use, collaborative community, and defensive capabilities make it a valuable asset for both offensive and defensive security efforts. It helps security professionals stay ahead of evolving threats and vulnerabilities, enabling them to protect systems and data effectively. In the ever-changing landscape of cybersecurity, Metasploit remains a trusted and essential tool for those dedicated to securing digital assets and networks.

Let's explore the key components and features that make the Metasploit Framework such a powerful and indispensable tool in the world of cybersecurity. At its heart, Metasploit is designed to streamline and enhance the penetration testing and vulnerability assessment process, making it an invaluable resource for security professionals.

The core of the Metasploit Framework consists of several essential components, each contributing to its effectiveness and versatility. These components work in harmony to facilitate the identification, exploitation, and remediation of vulnerabilities.

The first core component is the Metasploit Console, which serves as the primary interface for interacting with the framework. It provides a command-line interface (CLI) where users can enter commands to initiate scans, run exploits, and perform various tasks. The console is the control center of Metasploit, where testers execute their penetration testing activities.

The Metasploit Database is another critical component, serving as the repository for information about vulnerabilities, exploits, payloads, and sessions. It stores data related to discovered vulnerabilities, providing a centralized location for organizing and managing assessment findings. The database enhances collaboration and reporting capabilities.

A vital aspect of the Metasploit Framework is its extensive library of modules. Modules are pre-packaged code components that perform specific tasks within the framework. There are three main types of modules: exploits, payloads, and auxiliary modules. Exploits are used to take advantage of vulnerabilities, payloads run on exploited systems, and auxiliary modules provide additional functionalities like scanning and reconnaissance.

Payloads, in particular, are a fundamental element of Metasploit. They are responsible for executing specific actions on the exploited system, such as opening a remote command shell, transferring files, or capturing system information. Payloads are customizable and adaptable, allowing testers to tailor their actions to the target environment.

The Metasploit Framework also includes an advanced scripting language known as Metasploit Scripting Language (MSF-Scripts). MSF-Scripts enable users to create custom scripts and automate various tasks within the framework. This scripting language extends Metasploit's flexibility, making it easier to develop custom modules and functionalities.

Moreover, Metasploit provides a comprehensive set of auxiliary modules that enhance its capabilities. These modules cover a wide range of functionalities, including network scanning, fingerprinting, brute-force attacks, and more. Security professionals can leverage these auxiliary modules to perform various tasks during penetration tests.

One standout feature of Metasploit is its expansive database of known vulnerabilities and exploits. This database, continually updated, contains information about vulnerabilities, including their severity, affected systems, and available exploits. Security professionals can search the database to identify relevant vulnerabilities and corresponding exploits for their assessments.

Metasploit's flexibility is a significant advantage, allowing users to adapt it to their specific needs. It supports multiple operating systems and platforms, ensuring compatibility with a diverse range of target systems. This versatility is essential for conducting penetration tests across various environments.

Collaboration and community engagement are integral to the Metasploit ecosystem. Users can contribute their exploits, modules, and payloads to the community, fostering innovation and the sharing of knowledge. This collaborative approach ensures that Metasploit remains up-to-date and effective in addressing emerging threats.

Metasploit's user-friendly interfaces contribute to its accessibility. In addition to the command-line interface, Metasploit provides a graphical user interface (GUI) called Armitage. The GUI simplifies the use of Metasploit for those who prefer a visual approach and may not have extensive programming skills.

Furthermore, Metasploit's reporting capabilities are crucial for documenting findings and communicating assessment results. It generates detailed reports that provide a clear overview of identified vulnerabilities, their potential impact, and recommended remediation steps. These reports are invaluable for conveying assessment findings to stakeholders and management.

Another notable feature of Metasploit is its extensibility. Security professionals can extend Metasploit's functionality by developing custom modules, scripts, and exploits. This extensibility allows users to tailor Metasploit to specific requirements and address unique challenges.

Metasploit's continuous development and updates, led by Rapid7, ensure that it remains a reliable and cutting-edge tool in the field of cybersecurity. Regular updates address emerging threats and vulnerabilities, ensuring that security professionals have access to the latest techniques and capabilities.

In summary, the Metasploit Framework encompasses a range of key components and features that make it an indispensable tool for security professionals. From its modular architecture and extensive library of modules to its collaborative community and reporting capabilities, Metasploit streamlines the penetration testing and vulnerability assessment process.

Its versatility, compatibility with various platforms, and support for scripting and automation make it accessible to users of varying skill levels. Metasploit's commitment to community-driven development ensures that it remains a dynamic and effective tool in the ever-evolving landscape of cybersecurity. Whether you're an experienced ethical hacker or just starting your journey in cybersecurity, Metasploit is a valuable asset in your toolkit for assessing and enhancing the security of computer systems and networks.

Chapter 5: Target Identification and Selection

Understanding target scope is a fundamental aspect of any penetration testing or ethical hacking endeavor, as it defines the boundaries and limits of the assessment. The term "scope" refers to the specific systems, applications, and networks that will be included in the assessment, and it plays a crucial role in determining the goals and objectives of the engagement.

Defining the target scope is akin to drawing the boundaries of a map; it helps testers navigate through the vast landscape of the target environment. The scope outlines what systems and assets are within the purview of the assessment and what areas should be excluded.

Scope definition is not a one-size-fits-all process; it requires careful consideration and collaboration with stakeholders. The first step is to establish clear and well-defined objectives for the assessment. What are the goals of the penetration test? What are you trying to achieve or discover?

These objectives guide the scope definition process. They help determine which systems and assets are critical to achieving the assessment's goals and which areas can be excluded. For example, if the primary objective is to identify vulnerabilities in a web application, the scope may include only that application and the servers hosting it.

Collaboration with stakeholders is essential because they possess critical insights into the organization's infrastructure and priorities. Stakeholders may include IT administrators, security teams, and business leaders who can provide valuable information about the target environment.

Once the objectives are clear and stakeholders are engaged, it's time to identify the systems and assets that fall within the scope. This involves creating an inventory of target systems, including IP addresses, hostnames, and any relevant network segments. It's important to have a comprehensive and up-to-date list to avoid overlooking critical components.

However, scope definition is not just about what's included; it also involves specifying what's excluded. Exclusion criteria are just as crucial as inclusion criteria. For example, certain systems may be excluded because they are mission-critical and cannot be disrupted during the assessment.

Additionally, organizations may have compliance requirements or legal constraints that dictate what can or cannot be assessed. For instance, some systems may contain sensitive data that cannot be included in the assessment without proper authorization and safeguards.

The scope should also consider the testing methodology. Will the assessment involve black-box testing, where testers have no prior knowledge of the target environment, or will it include white-box testing, where testers have access to detailed information about the systems being assessed? This decision impacts the depth and breadth of the assessment.

Furthermore, the scope should account for any rules of engagement (ROE) that dictate how the assessment should be conducted. ROE may include guidelines for testing hours, communication protocols, and emergency procedures in case something goes wrong during the assessment.

One essential aspect of scope definition is the delineation between authorized and unauthorized activities. It's crucial to obtain proper authorization from the organization's decision-makers before conducting any penetration testing activities. Unauthorized testing can lead to legal consequences and disrupt business operations.

As part of scope definition, it's also advisable to establish a clear communication plan. This plan outlines how testers will communicate with stakeholders during the assessment, report findings, and address any issues that arise. Effective communication ensures that everyone is on the same page throughout the assessment.

Scope validation is another critical step. Once the scope is defined, it should be reviewed and validated to ensure that it aligns with the objectives and requirements of the assessment. Any discrepancies or ambiguities should be addressed before the testing begins.

Throughout the assessment, it's important to maintain strict adherence to the defined scope. Deviating from the scope can lead to unintended consequences, disrupt operations, and erode trust with stakeholders. Any changes to the scope should be documented, communicated, and authorized by relevant parties.

In summary, defining target scope is a foundational step in any penetration testing or ethical hacking engagement. It establishes the boundaries, objectives, and limits of the assessment, guiding testers as they navigate the target environment. Collaboration with stakeholders, clear objectives, comprehensive inventory, and adherence to rules of engagement are essential elements of effective scope definition. By defining the scope accurately and responsibly, security professionals can conduct assessments that provide valuable insights into an organization's security posture while minimizing risks and disruptions.

Navigating the legal and ethical considerations in the realm of penetration testing and ethical hacking is crucial for maintaining integrity and avoiding potential legal consequences. As we delve into this topic, it's important to recognize that these activities, although conducted with good intentions, can sometimes tread on legal and ethical gray areas.

First and foremost, it's essential to understand that engaging in penetration testing or ethical hacking without proper authorization is not only unethical but also illegal in many jurisdictions. Unauthorized access to computer systems, networks, or data constitutes a breach of law, and individuals or organizations involved can face severe legal consequences.

Obtaining explicit and written authorization from the target organization or system owner is a fundamental requirement before conducting any penetration testing activities. This authorization, often referred to as a "letter of engagement" or "permission to test," outlines the scope, objectives, and rules of engagement for the assessment.

Ethical hackers and penetration testers must adhere to the terms and conditions specified in the authorization letter diligently. Deviating from the agreed-upon scope or rules can lead to misunderstandings, damage, and potential legal action. Open and transparent communication with stakeholders is essential throughout the engagement.

One critical aspect of ethical hacking and penetration testing is the principle of informed consent. Individuals or organizations whose systems are being tested must be aware of and consent to the assessment. It's crucial to inform them about the potential risks, disruptions, and impacts of the assessment on their operations.

In some cases, organizations may have specific legal requirements or industry regulations that govern penetration testing activities. For instance, the General Data Protection Regulation (GDPR) in Europe imposes strict data protection and privacy requirements. Testers must ensure compliance with such regulations and obtain any necessary approvals.

Maintaining the confidentiality and privacy of sensitive data encountered during penetration testing is a paramount ethical consideration. Testers may encounter sensitive information, such as customer data, financial records, or proprietary information, during their assessments. Safeguarding this data is not only a legal requirement but also an ethical obligation.

Furthermore, ethical hackers and penetration testers should refrain from causing undue harm or disruption during their assessments. The goal is to identify vulnerabilities and weaknesses, not to exploit them for malicious purposes. Unintentional damage to systems, data loss, or service disruptions should be minimized and reported promptly.

Ethical hackers must approach their work with a mindset of responsible disclosure. This means promptly reporting identified vulnerabilities to the organization or system owner and providing sufficient information to allow them to remediate the issues. Public disclosure of vulnerabilities should only occur after adequate time has been given for remediation.

The disclosure process should adhere to a responsible and coordinated approach to ensure that vulnerabilities are addressed without putting the organization at risk. Testers should avoid "full disclosure" by publicly sharing all details of a vulnerability without allowing the organization time to fix it, as this can lead to exploitation by malicious actors.

Another ethical consideration is the use of information and tools obtained during penetration testing. Testers should use their knowledge and tools exclusively for the purpose of the assessment and not for personal gain or any other unauthorized activities. Sharing sensitive information or tools with unauthorized individuals is unethical and can have legal repercussions.

In addition to legal and ethical considerations, testers should be mindful of the potential impact of their activities on third parties. Sometimes, vulnerabilities may be present in third-party systems or services connected to the target organization. Testers must exercise caution to avoid unintended consequences on these external entities.

Testers should also respect the boundaries of the agreed-upon scope and avoid "going rogue" by testing systems or assets not covered by the authorization letter. Unauthorized testing can lead to legal issues and harm the reputation of the ethical hacker and their organization.

In summary, navigating the legal and ethical considerations of penetration testing and ethical hacking is an essential aspect of maintaining professionalism and integrity in this field. Proper authorization, informed consent, compliance with legal requirements, responsible disclosure, data privacy, and responsible use of knowledge and tools are key principles that ethical hackers and penetration testers must uphold. By adhering to these principles, professionals can conduct assessments that enhance security while minimizing legal and ethical risks.

Chapter 6: Port Scanning and Service Enumeration

Exploring the world of port scanning techniques is an essential aspect of understanding network reconnaissance and vulnerability assessment. Port scanning is a foundational process in penetration testing and ethical hacking, allowing professionals to identify open ports, services, and potential entry points into a target system or network.

At its core, port scanning is the act of systematically querying a target system or network to discover which network ports are open and responding to requests. Ports serve as communication endpoints that enable data to flow between devices, and identifying open ports is the first step in understanding a system's network configuration.

One of the most straightforward and commonly used port scanning techniques is known as the "TCP connect scan." In this method, the scanner attempts to establish a full TCP connection with each port of the target system. If a connection is successful, it indicates that the port is open, while a connection refusal signifies a closed port. TCP connect scans provide reliable results but are relatively slow and easily detectable by intrusion detection systems (IDS).

Another widely employed technique is the "TCP SYN scan," also known as "half-open scanning." In a SYN scan, the scanner sends a TCP SYN packet to the target ports. If the port is open, the target system responds with a SYN-ACK packet, confirming the connection request. If the port is closed, the system responds with a RST (reset) packet, indicating that the port is closed. SYN scans are faster than TCP connect scans and are less likely to be logged by target systems.

UDP scanning is another category of port scanning techniques that focuses on User Datagram Protocol (UDP) ports. UDP is a connectionless protocol, and scanning UDP ports is more challenging than scanning TCP ports because there is no built-in mechanism for confirming open ports. In UDP scanning, the scanner sends UDP packets to target ports and analyzes the responses. Lack of response indicates an open port, while ICMP "port unreachable" messages signify a closed port.

The "TCP FIN scan" is a stealthy technique that involves sending TCP FIN packets to target ports. If a port is open, it should ignore the FIN packet, and the scanner receives no response. If a port is closed, the target system typically responds with a RST packet. TCP FIN scans are used to determine whether a system follows the RFC 793 specification for handling FIN packets.

The "XMAS scan" is another stealthy technique that sends TCP packets with the FIN, URG, and PSH flags set. If a port is open, it often responds differently to these unusual packets than to regular packets, allowing the scanner to identify open ports. XMAS scans are stealthy but may not work against all target systems.

A more advanced technique is the "ACK scan," which focuses on determining whether a target system is stateful or stateless regarding its filtering rules. In an ACK scan, the scanner sends TCP ACK packets to target ports. If the target system responds with a RST packet, it indicates that the port is unfiltered. If the system does not respond, it suggests that the port is filtered, and the scanner cannot determine its state.

"Idle scanning" is a technique that leverages the characteristics of a zombie host to scan a target system while remaining stealthy. The scanner sends spoofed packets to the zombie host, which then sends packets to the target on behalf of the scanner. This approach can help mask the identity of the true scanner.

A variation of idle scanning is the "fragmentation scan," which involves sending fragmented packets to target ports. Fragmentation can sometimes bypass network filters and security devices, making it challenging for them to detect or block the scan.

"Version detection" is an extension of traditional port scanning techniques. It aims to identify the specific services and their versions running on open ports. Version detection relies on examining the responses received from the target system and comparing them to known service signatures and banners.

The choice of port scanning technique depends on several factors, including the desired level of stealth, the target environment, and the scanner's goals. Ethical hackers and penetration testers must carefully select the appropriate technique based on the circumstances of the assessment.

It's important to note that while port scanning is a valuable tool for network reconnaissance, it can also raise security alarms. Target systems and network security devices, such as firewalls and IDS, may detect and log port scanning activities. To mitigate this, ethical hackers often employ techniques to reduce the visibility of their scans or conduct them in a controlled and authorized manner.

In summary, port scanning techniques are a crucial part of network reconnaissance and vulnerability assessment. They enable security professionals to identify open ports, services, and potential vulnerabilities in target systems. However, it's essential to use these techniques responsibly and within the bounds of legal and ethical considerations. By carefully selecting the appropriate scanning technique and approach, ethical hackers can gather valuable information while minimizing the risk of detection and disruption.

Exploring the realm of service enumeration methods is essential for understanding how ethical hackers and penetration testers identify and gather information about the services running on target systems. Service enumeration is a critical phase in the process of network reconnaissance, as it provides insights into the specific software and protocols in use, potentially revealing vulnerabilities and attack vectors.

Service enumeration can be thought of as the process of discovering and identifying the various network services that a target system offers. These services could include web servers, email servers, file transfer protocols, database servers, and more. Knowing what services are running on a system is a fundamental step in assessing its security posture.

One of the most straightforward methods of service enumeration is banner grabbing. Banner grabbing involves connecting to a target port and examining the banner or banner-like information that the service provides upon connection. This information often includes the service name, version, and sometimes even the operating system it's running on. Banner grabbing is non-intrusive and relies on publicly available information.

Another commonly used method is the Transmission Control Protocol (TCP) handshake, which is part of the three-way handshake process used to establish a TCP connection. By sending a SYN (synchronize) packet to a target port and analyzing the response, ethical hackers can determine whether the port is open and may gain information about the service.

In addition to banner grabbing and the TCP handshake, service enumeration can involve sending specific queries or commands to services known to run on particular ports. For example, querying the Hypertext Transfer Protocol (HTTP) service on port 80 may involve sending an HTTP GET request to retrieve a web page. Analyzing the response can provide insights into the web server software, its version, and potentially the technologies used on the website.

Similarly, querying the Domain Name System (DNS) service on port 53 can involve requesting information about domain names or querying for specific DNS records. The responses received during DNS enumeration can reveal information about the domain structure, mail servers, and other DNS-related details.

The Simple Network Management Protocol (SNMP) is often used for managing and monitoring network devices. Ethical hackers may employ SNMP enumeration to gather information about network devices, such as routers, switches, and printers. SNMP queries can reveal details like device names, configurations, and even potentially sensitive information if the default community strings are known.

Port scanning tools, such as Nmap, provide robust service enumeration capabilities. Nmap can perform version detection by sending probes to open ports and comparing the responses to its extensive database of service fingerprints. This method allows ethical hackers to identify the specific services, versions, and sometimes even potential vulnerabilities present on target systems.

While these methods are useful for service enumeration, it's important to exercise caution and adhere to ethical guidelines. Unauthorized probing or excessive queries can lead to disruptions and potentially legal issues. Ethical hackers should always obtain proper authorization before conducting service enumeration activities.

Sometimes, service enumeration may involve techniques to bypass security mechanisms, such as firewalls or intrusion detection systems. Techniques like firewall evasion and tunneling can be used to sneak queries past network defenses, allowing ethical hackers to gain insights into services that might otherwise be hidden.

Service enumeration is not limited to identifying services on a single host. Ethical hackers often perform service discovery across entire networks or subnets. They use tools and techniques to scan multiple hosts in a network range simultaneously, efficiently collecting information about the services running on numerous systems.

The choice of service enumeration method depends on various factors, including the target environment, the desired level of detail, and the ethical hacker's goals. Each method has its advantages and limitations, and a combination of techniques may be employed to obtain a comprehensive view of the target environment.

In summary, service enumeration methods are a vital component of network reconnaissance and vulnerability assessment. They empower ethical hackers and penetration testers to identify and gather information about the services running on target systems, aiding in the discovery of potential vulnerabilities and attack vectors. Responsible and authorized service enumeration is a crucial step in assessing the security posture of systems and networks while adhering to ethical and legal standards.

Chapter 7: Exploiting Common Network Vulnerabilities

Let's delve into the world of common network vulnerabilities, as understanding these weaknesses is essential for anyone involved in cybersecurity, penetration testing, or network defense. Network vulnerabilities represent weaknesses in a network's security posture that can be exploited by malicious actors to gain unauthorized access, disrupt operations, or steal sensitive information.

One of the most prevalent network vulnerabilities is the misconfiguration of network devices and services. These misconfigurations can range from using default usernames and passwords on network devices to improperly configuring access control lists (ACLs) or firewall rules. Misconfigured devices and services can provide attackers with easy entry points into a network.

Another common vulnerability is the lack of regular software updates and patch management. Outdated operating systems and software are susceptible to known vulnerabilities that attackers can exploit. Keeping systems up-to-date with security patches is critical to closing these vulnerabilities and reducing the attack surface.

Weak or easily guessable passwords are a perennial problem in network security. Passwords like "123456" or "password" are still prevalent, and attackers often use password cracking techniques to gain access to accounts. Implementing strong password policies, multi-factor authentication, and regular password changes can help mitigate this vulnerability.

Unsecured network protocols are another area of concern. Some older protocols, like Telnet and FTP, transmit data in plain text, making it easy for attackers to intercept and eavesdrop on sensitive information. Using secure alternatives, such as SSH and SFTP, helps protect data in transit.

Network services that are unnecessarily exposed can be a significant vulnerability. Services like Remote Desktop Protocol (RDP) or administrative interfaces should only be accessible from trusted networks or through secure VPN connections. Exposing them to the public internet increases the risk of unauthorized access and exploitation.

Inadequate network segmentation is a vulnerability that can lead to lateral movement by attackers. Networks should be divided into segments or zones with strict access controls to limit the spread of attacks. A flat or poorly segmented network can allow attackers to move laterally from one compromised system to another.

Unpatched or unhardened network devices, such as routers, switches, and firewalls, can present vulnerabilities. These devices may have default settings or vulnerabilities that attackers can exploit to gain control or disrupt network traffic. Regularly updating firmware and configuring devices securely are essential steps in reducing this risk.

Denial-of-Service (DoS) and Distributed Denial-of-Service (DDoS) attacks are persistent threats that can overwhelm network resources, rendering them unavailable to legitimate users. Insufficient mitigation measures in place to handle these attacks can leave a network vulnerable to service disruption.

Social engineering attacks targeting employees are a vulnerability that often goes underestimated. Phishing emails, phone calls, and pretexting can trick users into revealing sensitive information or executing malicious actions. Educating users about these threats and implementing security awareness training programs can help mitigate this risk.

Insecure or outdated network protocols, such as the use of outdated encryption algorithms or SSL/TLS configurations, can expose networks to vulnerabilities. Attackers may exploit weaknesses in encryption to intercept and decrypt sensitive data. Employing strong encryption protocols and configurations is essential for securing data in transit.

Open ports and services on network devices can be an entry point for attackers. Ports that are not necessary for business operations should be closed or filtered to reduce the attack surface. Regularly conducting port scans and vulnerability assessments can help identify and remediate open ports and services.

Insufficient network monitoring and intrusion detection capabilities represent a significant vulnerability. Without real-time monitoring, organizations may not detect unauthorized access or suspicious activities until it's too late. Implementing robust monitoring solutions and intrusion detection systems is essential for identifying and responding to security incidents.

Weak access controls and inadequate privilege management can lead to unauthorized access and data breaches. Users should only have the permissions necessary for their roles, and access to sensitive systems or data should be restricted and closely monitored.

Lastly, inadequate backup and disaster recovery procedures can leave a network vulnerable to data loss and extended downtime in the event of a cyberattack or hardware failure. Regularly backing up critical data and testing disaster recovery plans helps organizations recover from incidents and minimize the impact.

In summary, common network vulnerabilities represent weaknesses that can be exploited by attackers to compromise network security. These vulnerabilities include misconfigurations, outdated software, weak passwords, unsecured protocols, exposed services, inadequate segmentation, and more. Addressing these vulnerabilities requires a comprehensive approach that includes regular patching, strong access controls, user education, and robust monitoring. By proactively identifying and mitigating these vulnerabilities, organizations can strengthen their network security posture and reduce the risk of cyberattacks.

Exploring the realm of exploitation techniques is essential for understanding the methods that malicious actors use to compromise systems and networks. Exploitation represents the act of taking advantage of vulnerabilities or weaknesses in software, hardware, or configurations to gain unauthorized access or control over a target system. Ethical hackers and penetration testers also study these techniques to understand how to defend against them and assess the security of systems and networks.

One commonly employed exploitation technique is the use of exploits, which are pieces of code or software specifically designed to target and take advantage of known vulnerabilities in applications or operating systems. Exploits can allow attackers to execute arbitrary code, gain access to sensitive information, or compromise the integrity and availability of a system.

Zero-day exploits are a subset of exploits that target vulnerabilities that are not publicly known or for which no security patches are available. These exploits can be particularly dangerous because they take advantage of vulnerabilities that have not yet been addressed by software vendors or security teams.

Phishing is another exploitation technique that leverages social engineering to deceive individuals into taking malicious actions. Phishing attacks often involve emails or messages that appear legitimate, prompting users to click on malicious links, download malware, or provide sensitive information, such as login credentials.

Social engineering attacks extend beyond phishing and can include tactics like pretexting, baiting, and tailgating. These techniques manipulate human psychology to gain unauthorized access or information, exploiting trust and naivety.

Malware, short for malicious software, is a broad category of software designed to compromise systems or networks. Exploitation often involves delivering malware to target systems through various means, such as email attachments, infected websites, or removable media. Malware can encompass viruses, worms, Trojans, ransomware, and more.

Remote code execution is a significant goal of many exploitation techniques. Attackers seek to execute their own code on a target system to gain control or perform malicious actions. This can include running arbitrary commands, installing backdoors, or escalating privileges to gain administrative access.

Privilege escalation is an exploitation technique that involves elevating one's level of access or privileges on a system or network. Attackers who gain initial access with limited privileges often seek ways to escalate their rights to perform more advanced attacks or compromise additional resources.

Exploiting misconfigurations is a common technique that takes advantage of security settings or configurations that are not properly implemented or updated. These misconfigurations can allow attackers to bypass security controls, access restricted resources, or gain unauthorized privileges.

Buffer overflow attacks are a specific type of exploitation technique that targets vulnerabilities in software code. By sending input data that exceeds the buffer's allocated memory space, attackers can overwrite adjacent memory and potentially execute arbitrary code. Buffer overflows can lead to system crashes, data corruption, and unauthorized code execution.

Man-in-the-middle (MitM) attacks involve intercepting and manipulating communication between two parties. Attackers position themselves between the communication path, allowing them to eavesdrop on sensitive information, alter messages, or inject malicious content. MitM attacks can target various communication channels, including Wi-Fi, email, and web traffic.

Credential theft and cracking are exploitation techniques aimed at acquiring and using login credentials. Attackers may use methods like brute force attacks or dictionary attacks to guess passwords or employ keyloggers to capture keystrokes. Once credentials are obtained, attackers can gain unauthorized access to accounts or systems.

Cross-Site Scripting (XSS) and Cross-Site Request Forgery (CSRF) are web application exploitation techniques. XSS involves injecting malicious scripts into web pages viewed by other users, potentially leading to the theft of sensitive information or session hijacking. CSRF tricks users into performing actions on web applications without their consent.

Exploitation techniques can also target vulnerabilities in network protocols. For example, the Address Resolution Protocol (ARP) spoofing technique manipulates ARP packets to associate an attacker's MAC address with a legitimate IP address, enabling network traffic interception and manipulation.

Distributed denial-of-service (DDoS) attacks are an exploitation technique that overwhelms a target system or network with a flood of traffic, rendering it inaccessible to legitimate users. DDoS attacks aim to disrupt services, cause downtime, or exhaust network resources.

Infiltration through physical access is an exploitation technique that involves gaining physical access to a target system or facility. Attackers may use tactics like lock picking, badge cloning, or impersonation to bypass physical security measures.

Exploitation techniques encompass a vast and evolving landscape of tactics and methods that malicious actors use to compromise systems and networks. Understanding these techniques is crucial for both offensive and defensive cybersecurity efforts. Ethical hackers and penetration testers study exploitation techniques to identify vulnerabilities and develop effective defenses, while security professionals work to implement protective measures that thwart potential attackers. Ultimately, the ongoing battle between exploitation and defense shapes the cybersecurity landscape and underscores the importance of proactive security practices.

Chapter 8: Post-Exploitation and Maintaining Access

Exploring post-exploitation strategies is a crucial aspect of understanding the complete lifecycle of a cyberattack. Once an attacker has successfully gained unauthorized access to a system or network, their objectives often extend beyond the initial breach. Post-exploitation refers to the phase of an attack where the attacker seeks to maintain access, gather valuable information, and further exploit the compromised environment.

One key goal of post-exploitation is maintaining persistent access. Attackers aim to ensure that even if their initial entry point is discovered and closed, they can still regain access to the compromised system or network. This is achieved through various means, such as planting backdoors, creating additional user accounts, or exploiting existing vulnerabilities.

Backdoors are a common post-exploitation technique used to maintain access. These are hidden or undocumented methods of accessing a system, allowing attackers to enter without going through the initial attack vector. Backdoors can be implemented as software, scripts, or configuration changes and are often difficult to detect.

Rootkits are another form of post-exploitation tool that attackers use to maintain control over a compromised system. Rootkits hide malicious activities and processes from security tools and administrators, making it challenging to detect and remove them. They often replace or modify system files and components.

Once attackers have established persistent access, they move on to data exfiltration. This involves stealing sensitive information from the compromised system or network. Attackers may target a variety of data, including personal identifiable information (PII), financial records, intellectual property, or login credentials.

Data exfiltration techniques can vary widely and may involve compressing and encrypting stolen data, disguising it within legitimate network traffic, or using covert channels to transmit information. Detection and prevention of data exfiltration are critical components of post-exploitation defense.

Privilege escalation is a post-exploitation strategy that attackers use to increase their level of access within a compromised system or network. Once inside, they seek ways to elevate their privileges from standard user accounts to administrative or root-level access, which grants them more control and capabilities.

Attackers may exploit known vulnerabilities or weaknesses in the operating system or applications to achieve privilege escalation. They may also abuse misconfigurations or weaknesses in access control mechanisms. Privilege escalation can provide attackers with the authority to make system-wide changes, install malware, or manipulate configurations.

Covering tracks is an essential aspect of post-exploitation. Attackers aim to erase or obfuscate evidence of their presence and actions to avoid detection and attribution. This includes cleaning up logs, erasing command histories, and deleting any traces of their activities on the compromised system.

Intrusion detection and prevention systems, as well as log analysis tools, play a crucial role in detecting post-exploitation activities. Security professionals actively monitor system logs, network traffic, and behavioral anomalies to identify signs of unauthorized access or suspicious behavior.

Some attackers use lateral movement techniques during post-exploitation to expand their reach within a network. Lateral movement involves moving from one compromised system to another to explore and exploit additional resources. Attackers may use stolen credentials, exploits, or legitimate remote management tools to traverse the network.

Post-exploitation can also involve privilege escalation on network devices, such as routers and switches, to gain control over network traffic and manipulate it for malicious purposes. This can include redirecting traffic, eavesdropping on communications, or launching further attacks on other systems.

Once attackers have accomplished their objectives, they may choose to exit the compromised environment. However, they often leave behind persistent access points or backdoors for future exploitation. Detecting and closing these access points is a critical part of post-incident response and remediation.

Ultimately, post-exploitation strategies are a dynamic and evolving aspect of cybersecurity. Attackers continually adapt and develop new techniques to maintain access, steal data, and cover their tracks. Security professionals must stay vigilant, employ proactive defenses, and actively monitor their networks to detect and respond to post-exploitation activities effectively. Understanding the adversary's post-exploitation mindset is essential for securing systems and networks against these persistent threats.

Exploring the concept of maintaining access and persistence in the realm of cybersecurity reveals a critical aspect of the attacker's mindset and a key challenge for defenders. Once an attacker successfully gains unauthorized access to a system or network, their primary objective often extends beyond the initial breach. They seek to maintain a foothold in the compromised environment, ensuring continued access and control over the targeted assets.

One of the primary techniques employed by attackers to maintain access is the creation of backdoors. These hidden or undocumented entry points into a system or network provide attackers with an alternate means of re-entry, even if their initial point of entry is discovered and closed. Backdoors can take the form of malicious software, scripts, or configuration changes and are designed to remain hidden from security controls and administrators.

Rootkits, a specialized form of backdoor, are particularly effective at maintaining persistence. These stealthy pieces of malware are designed to hide malicious activities and processes from detection. Rootkits often replace or modify critical system files and components to cloak their presence and ensure that they continue running undetected.

Attackers may also establish additional user accounts or elevate the privileges of existing accounts during the post-exploitation phase. Privilege escalation is a technique that allows attackers to gain higher levels of access within a compromised system or network. By achieving administrative or root-level access, attackers can exert greater control and influence over the targeted environment.

Persistence can be achieved through various means, including modifying system configurations to execute malicious code during system startup or login. This ensures that the attacker's tools and backdoors are automatically activated each time the compromised system is rebooted or a user logs in.

Another technique employed by attackers is the use of scheduled tasks or cron jobs to execute malicious scripts or commands at predetermined intervals. These scheduled activities can facilitate ongoing access and control, allowing attackers to perform actions at specific times or in response to specific triggers.

Some attackers leverage legitimate remote management and administration tools that are already present on the compromised system or network. By using these tools, they can maintain access without arousing suspicion, as the tools are part of normal system operations. This tactic can make it challenging for defenders to distinguish between legitimate and malicious activity.

Persistence is not limited to individual systems; attackers often seek to establish persistence within a network. They may compromise network devices such as routers, switches, or firewalls to manipulate network traffic, redirect data, or maintain control over critical infrastructure. This can enable them to monitor communications, intercept sensitive data, or launch further attacks on other systems.

To defend against these post-exploitation tactics, security professionals employ various strategies and tools. Intrusion detection systems and advanced threat detection solutions are crucial components of an organization's cybersecurity arsenal. These systems monitor network and system activities for signs of malicious behavior, helping to detect and respond to post-exploitation activities in real-time.

Security professionals also conduct regular security audits and vulnerability assessments to proactively identify and remediate weaknesses that could be exploited by attackers. Patch management and software updates are essential to keep systems and applications secure by addressing known vulnerabilities.

Implementing strong access controls and privilege management practices can help prevent attackers from escalating their privileges and maintaining access. Regularly reviewing and adjusting user permissions, as well as enforcing the principle of least privilege, limits the attacker's ability to move freely within the compromised environment.

Effective incident response procedures are critical for organizations to respond promptly and decisively when post-exploitation activities are detected. Having a well-defined incident response plan in place can minimize the impact of an attack, facilitate the identification and removal of backdoors, and help organizations recover more swiftly.

Furthermore, organizations should consider employing security information and event management (SIEM) systems to centralize log data and enable proactive threat hunting. SIEM solutions provide security teams with the ability to correlate and analyze events across the entire network, enhancing their ability to detect and respond to post-exploitation activities.

While attackers continually adapt and evolve their tactics to maintain access and persistence, security professionals must remain vigilant and proactive in their efforts to defend against these threats. Understanding the attacker's mindset and the techniques they employ is crucial for developing effective cybersecurity strategies and staying one step ahead of evolving threats. By investing in robust defenses, monitoring capabilities, and incident response readiness, organizations can bolster their resilience against post-exploitation activities and protect their valuable assets.

Chapter 9: Evading Detection and Covering Tracks

Exploring the realm of evading detection techniques in the context of cybersecurity reveals a cat-and-mouse game between attackers and defenders, where the goal of attackers is to remain undetected while carrying out their malicious activities. Evading detection involves a range of strategies and tactics employed by malicious actors to bypass security measures and avoid raising suspicion.

One fundamental evasion technique is the use of obfuscation. Attackers often employ obfuscation to disguise the true nature of their activities, making it difficult for security tools and analysts to recognize malicious patterns. Obfuscation techniques can involve encrypting malware, encoding command and control communications, or renaming malicious files to appear benign.

Polymorphic malware is a sophisticated form of obfuscation where the malware code changes its appearance each time it infects a new system. This dynamic behavior allows the malware to evade signature-based detection, as traditional antivirus software relies on known patterns or signatures to identify threats.

Another common evasion technique is the use of encryption to protect malicious communication channels. Attackers encrypt data exchanged between compromised systems and command and control servers, making it challenging for network monitoring solutions to inspect and detect malicious traffic.

Steganography is a technique that involves hiding malicious data within innocent-looking files or images. By embedding malicious code or data within legitimate files, attackers can evade detection while transmitting malware or exfiltrating data. Steganography makes it difficult to identify malicious content based on file signatures alone.

Intrusion detection and prevention systems (IDS/IPS) are essential components of network security. To evade these systems, attackers may fragment or encrypt their network traffic to obscure their activities. By breaking data into smaller, seemingly harmless pieces or encrypting it, attackers can bypass network-based detection mechanisms.

Fileless malware is a particularly stealthy evasion technique. This type of malware operates entirely in memory, leaving no traces on the file system. Since traditional antivirus solutions primarily scan files on disk, they often struggle to detect fileless malware, which resides solely in RAM.

Attackers also employ evasion techniques that target endpoint security solutions. They may tamper with antivirus software, disable security services, or manipulate security settings to disable or weaken protection mechanisms. This allows them to carry out their activities without interference from endpoint security tools.

Living-off-the-land (LotL) is a technique where attackers use legitimate system tools and utilities to carry out malicious activities. By leveraging built-in tools such as PowerShell, Windows Management Instrumentation (WMI), or command-line interfaces, attackers can avoid raising suspicion, as these tools are commonly used for legitimate purposes.

Rootkits, previously mentioned in the context of maintaining access, can also serve as evasion tools.

Rootkits not only hide malicious activities but can also manipulate system behaviors and responses to evade detection by security software.

Anti-forensics techniques are employed by attackers to erase or manipulate digital footprints. Attackers may delete logs, alter timestamps, or modify event records to cover their tracks and hinder forensic investigations. These tactics make it difficult for incident responders to reconstruct the timeline of an attack.

Evasion techniques can also target behavioral analysis and anomaly detection. Attackers may mimic normal user behavior to avoid triggering alarms or alerts. By acting inconspicuously and avoiding suspicious actions, they can stay under the radar of security monitoring systems.

Another evasion strategy is to blend in with legitimate traffic. Attackers may use known and trusted communication protocols, such as HTTP or DNS, to hide their activities within the vast volume of legitimate traffic on a network. This tactic can make it challenging to identify malicious behavior based solely on network traffic patterns.

To detect and counter these evasion techniques, security professionals employ a combination of strategies and technologies. Signature-based detection systems are effective at identifying known threats, but they may struggle against polymorphic malware and zero-day exploits.

Behavioral analysis and anomaly detection are essential for identifying suspicious activities that deviate from established baselines. These systems monitor user and system behavior to detect unusual patterns that may indicate an attack.

Security information and event management (SIEM) solutions play a crucial role in aggregating and analyzing data from various sources to identify potential threats. By correlating data and events across the network, SIEMs help security teams detect evasive tactics and respond effectively.

Sandboxing and threat emulation technologies provide a controlled environment for executing suspicious files and code. By observing how these elements behave in isolation, security teams can identify malicious activities that might otherwise go undetected.

Machine learning and artificial intelligence (AI) are increasingly used to enhance detection capabilities. These technologies can analyze large datasets, identify patterns, and detect deviations from normal behavior, making them valuable tools for spotting evasive techniques.

Effective cybersecurity relies on a multi-layered approach that combines signature-based detection with behavioral analysis, anomaly detection, and the use of advanced technologies like AI. Staying informed about emerging evasion techniques and continually adapting security strategies is essential to stay ahead of attackers in the ever-evolving landscape of cybersecurity.

Exploring the concept of covering tracks and removing evidence in the realm of cybersecurity uncovers a critical aspect of an attacker's strategy — the effort to conceal their presence and actions after compromising a system or network. This phase of an attack, often referred to as "post-incident cleanup" or "covering tracks," is a crucial component of the attacker's playbook, and it poses a significant challenge for defenders and incident responders.

Covering tracks encompasses a range of tactics and techniques aimed at erasing or obfuscating digital footprints left behind during an attack. Attackers understand that traceable evidence, if left unchecked, can lead to their identification and the attribution of the attack. To avoid detection and legal consequences, they employ various methods to obscure their activities.

One fundamental aspect of covering tracks involves the manipulation or deletion of log files. Logs are records of system and network activities, including login attempts, file access, and application usage. Attackers may alter or delete these logs to remove any evidence of their presence or actions. By doing so, they hinder the ability of security teams to reconstruct the timeline of the attack.

Intrusion detection systems (IDS) and security information and event management (SIEM) solutions play a significant role in monitoring network and system activities. They rely on log data to detect and alert on suspicious behavior. Deleting or tampering with logs can disrupt the detection process and buy attackers more time to remain undetected.

Event log manipulation can involve altering timestamps to make it appear as though certain actions occurred at different times or modifying event records to remove any references to the attacker's activities. These tactics add confusion to forensic investigations and hinder the efforts of incident responders.

Attackers may also target system artifacts that store evidence of their actions. Temporary files, cache data, and registry entries often contain traces of an attacker's presence. By removing or obfuscating these artifacts, attackers reduce the likelihood of detection. Security professionals must conduct thorough forensic analysis to identify and recover such artifacts.

Rootkits, previously discussed in the context of maintaining access, are versatile tools that can be used for both evasion and covering tracks. They can hide malicious processes, files, and registry entries, making it exceedingly difficult for investigators to discover evidence of an attack. Rootkits often operate at the kernel level, where they have privileged access to the system, allowing them to manipulate data and processes with ease.

To further obscure their actions, attackers may employ anti-forensics techniques. These techniques involve methods to thwart or hinder forensic analysis. Anti-forensics may include encryption of stored data, the use of file shredding tools to securely delete files, and overwriting free disk space to remove traces of deleted files.

Encryption of stored data is an effective anti-forensics technique because it renders data unreadable without the decryption key. Attackers may encrypt files or data that contain sensitive information about their activities, making it virtually impossible for forensic investigators to extract meaningful evidence.

File shredding tools overwrite data multiple times with random patterns, making it extremely challenging to recover deleted files through traditional forensic methods. Attackers may use these tools to securely delete files they no longer require, ensuring that no remnants of their actions linger.

Overwriting free disk space is a technique that involves writing random data to the unused portions of a storage device, effectively erasing any traces of previously deleted files. By doing so, attackers ensure that even if deleted files were not securely erased, they cannot be easily recovered.

Attackers may also use cover stories or misinformation to misdirect investigators. By planting false clues or fabricating alternative explanations for security incidents, they divert attention away from their actual activities. This tactic can lead investigators down false paths, wasting valuable time and resources.

Covering tracks is not limited to digital manipulation; it also includes efforts to physically remove or alter evidence. Attackers may attempt to remove physical devices or media that contain incriminating data. For example, they might steal a compromised hard drive or USB device to eliminate any possibility of forensic analysis.

Security professionals and incident responders employ various countermeasures to counter these covering track techniques. One essential approach is proactive logging and monitoring. Security teams maintain logs in tamper-evident formats and store them in secure locations or offsite to prevent unauthorized access or deletion.

Immutable logs, which cannot be modified or deleted, are another valuable tool. These logs provide a tamper-resistant record of system and network activities, ensuring that evidence remains intact for forensic analysis.

Network segmentation and access controls limit an attacker's ability to move freely within a network. Implementing these measures can help contain an attack and reduce the scope of potential evidence tampering.

Intrusion detection and prevention systems (IDS/IPS) are deployed to monitor network traffic and detect malicious activities. These systems can generate alerts when they identify potential evidence tampering or evasion techniques.

Effective incident response procedures are critical for organizations to follow when an attack is suspected or detected. Incident response teams must be well-trained and equipped to investigate and mitigate security incidents, including those involving covering tracks.

In summary, covering tracks and removing evidence are integral components of an attacker's strategy to evade detection and attribution. Attackers employ a range of tactics to manipulate logs, alter timestamps, delete files, and obscure their actions. Security professionals and incident responders must stay vigilant, employ tamper-evident logging practices, and be prepared to conduct thorough forensic investigations to uncover evidence of attacks and identify responsible actors. In the ever-evolving landscape of cybersecurity, understanding these evasion techniques is essential for defenders to stay one step ahead of attackers and safeguard critical assets.

Chapter 10: Reporting and Best Practices

Exploring the importance of comprehensive reporting guidelines in the field of cybersecurity unveils a critical aspect of incident response and management. Reporting plays a pivotal role in ensuring that security incidents and breaches are properly documented, analyzed, and addressed in a structured and organized manner. In an era where cyber threats continue to evolve and grow in complexity, the ability to provide clear and comprehensive reports is essential for organizations to effectively mitigate risks and learn from security incidents.

One of the primary objectives of comprehensive reporting is to document the details of a security incident accurately. This includes capturing critical information such as the nature of the incident, the scope of the impact, the assets involved, and the tactics, techniques, and procedures (TTPs) employed by the attackers. Accurate reporting lays the foundation for understanding the incident and formulating an effective response strategy.

Timeliness is a key consideration when it comes to reporting security incidents. Organizations must establish guidelines and procedures that specify how quickly incidents should be reported once they are detected. Rapid reporting is essential for swift containment and mitigation, as well as for meeting legal and regulatory requirements, which often stipulate specific reporting deadlines.

Clarity and consistency are fundamental aspects of comprehensive reporting guidelines. Reports should be structured in a standardized format that is easy to follow and understand. This ensures that all relevant information is captured, and nothing important is overlooked. Consistency in reporting facilitates comparison and analysis of incidents over time, aiding in the identification of patterns and trends.

Effective communication is a critical component of comprehensive reporting. Security professionals must convey technical details and findings in a clear and concise manner that can be understood by a range of stakeholders, including executives, legal teams, and technical staff. Reports should avoid jargon and technical language that may be confusing to non-technical readers.

An important consideration in comprehensive reporting is data privacy and confidentiality. Organizations must strike a balance between sharing information for analysis and protecting sensitive data. Reporting guidelines should include procedures for handling and redacting sensitive information to ensure compliance with data protection regulations and industry standards.

Comprehensive reporting goes beyond documenting the incident itself; it also includes capturing the actions taken during the incident response process. This includes the steps taken to contain the incident, the tools and techniques used for analysis, and the decisions made by incident response teams. These details are invaluable for assessing the effectiveness of the response and refining incident response procedures.

Another critical aspect of reporting is the identification of root causes and contributing factors. Understanding why an incident occurred and what vulnerabilities or weaknesses were exploited is essential for preventing future incidents. Reporting guidelines should encourage a thorough analysis of the incident's causes and provide a framework for making recommendations for remediation and prevention.

Compliance with legal and regulatory requirements is a significant driver for comprehensive reporting. Many industries and jurisdictions have specific reporting mandates for data breaches and security incidents. Organizations must ensure that their reporting guidelines align with these requirements to avoid legal consequences and regulatory penalties.

Beyond compliance, comprehensive reporting serves as a valuable tool for risk management and decision-making. Reports provide insights into the impact of security incidents on an organization's operations, reputation, and financial health. This information helps leadership make informed decisions about resource allocation, cybersecurity investments, and strategic planning.

Continuous improvement is a core principle of cybersecurity, and reporting plays a vital role in this process. Incident reports should not be seen as static documents but as living records that contribute to organizational learning. By analyzing incident reports and identifying areas for improvement, organizations can enhance their security posture and resilience against future threats.

Effective reporting also extends to external stakeholders, such as law enforcement agencies, regulatory bodies, and affected parties. Reporting guidelines should include procedures for sharing information with these entities when required. Collaboration with law enforcement, in particular, can be instrumental in investigating and prosecuting cybercriminals.

A comprehensive incident report typically includes the following elements:

Incident Overview: A concise summary of the incident, including the date and time of detection, the affected assets, and a brief description of the incident's nature.

Incident Details: A more detailed account of the incident, including the timeline of events, the techniques used by the attackers, and any indicators of compromise (IoCs) discovered.

Impact Assessment: An evaluation of the impact of the incident on the organization, including financial losses, operational disruptions, and reputational damage.

Response Actions: A description of the actions taken during the incident response process, including containment, eradication, and recovery efforts.

Root Cause Analysis: An examination of the underlying causes and contributing factors that led to the incident, with recommendations for remediation.

Lessons Learned: Reflections on what the organization can learn from the incident and how it can improve its security posture and incident response procedures.

Recommendations: Specific actions and measures to prevent similar incidents in the future, which may include changes to policies, procedures, or security controls.

Appendices: Additional documentation, such as technical logs, forensic findings, and incident response team notes, that support the report's findings and conclusions.

Comprehensive reporting guidelines should be adaptable and flexible to accommodate different types of incidents and organizations' specific needs. They should also include provisions for reporting to external parties, as required by law or industry regulations.

In summary, comprehensive reporting guidelines are a cornerstone of effective incident response and cybersecurity management. They ensure that incidents are documented accurately and thoroughly, facilitate communication among stakeholders, and support risk management and continuous improvement efforts. By following well-defined reporting guidelines, organizations can enhance their resilience against cyber threats and minimize the impact of security incidents on their operations and reputation.

Exploring best practices in network reconnaissance reveals a foundational aspect of cybersecurity that is essential for understanding and defending against potential threats. Network reconnaissance, often referred to as information gathering or discovery, is the initial phase of a cyberattack where adversaries seek to gather intelligence about a target network or system. To effectively defend against these reconnaissance efforts, organizations must employ best practices that enhance their situational awareness, detect suspicious activities, and bolster their overall security posture.

One fundamental best practice in network reconnaissance is the establishment of a clear and comprehensive network inventory. Organizations should maintain an up-to-date record of all assets, including servers, workstations, network devices, applications, and services. This inventory serves as the foundation for understanding the network's structure and identifying potential vulnerabilities.

Asset discovery tools and automated scanning solutions can assist organizations in building and maintaining their network inventories. These tools provide real-time visibility into the network and help identify any rogue or unauthorized devices that may be present.

Active monitoring and continuous scanning of the network are critical best practices for detecting unauthorized reconnaissance activities. Security teams should employ intrusion detection systems (IDS) and intrusion prevention systems (IPS) to monitor network traffic for suspicious patterns or anomalies. These systems can generate alerts when they detect activities indicative of reconnaissance attempts, such as port scans or unusual login attempts.

Regularly reviewing and analyzing network traffic logs is another essential practice for detecting reconnaissance activities. By examining log data, security professionals can identify patterns and behaviors that may indicate malicious intent. Anomalous login patterns, repeated failed login attempts, or unusual access to sensitive resources can all be signs of reconnaissance efforts.

Security information and event management (SIEM) solutions play a crucial role in centralizing and analyzing log data from various sources. These solutions enable security teams to correlate events and identify potential reconnaissance activities by aggregating data and applying analytics.

Organizations should also implement robust access controls and segmentation practices to limit the exposure of critical assets to potential attackers. Access controls help ensure that only authorized users can access specific resources, reducing the attack surface and making it more challenging for adversaries to gather information about the network.

Segmenting the network into separate zones or virtual LANs (VLANs) based on security requirements can further restrict lateral movement for attackers. Even if an adversary gains a foothold in one part of the network, segmentation can prevent them from easily moving to other areas.

Regular vulnerability assessments and penetration testing are integral to best practices in network reconnaissance. By proactively identifying and addressing vulnerabilities in the network, organizations can mitigate the risk of exploitation. Vulnerability assessments involve scanning the network for known vulnerabilities, while penetration testing simulates real-world attacks to assess the network's security posture.

Security professionals should stay informed about emerging threats and reconnaissance techniques through threat intelligence sources. By understanding the tactics, techniques, and procedures (TTPs) employed by adversaries, organizations can tailor their defenses and detection mechanisms to thwart reconnaissance efforts effectively.

Network monitoring and anomaly detection should extend to external threats as well. Organizations should deploy intrusion detection and prevention systems at network borders and firewalls to identify and block suspicious traffic originating from the internet.

Implementing honeypots and deception technologies can also be an effective practice for deterring reconnaissance activities. Honeypots are decoy systems designed to attract and divert attackers away from critical assets.

When adversaries interact with honeypots, security teams gain valuable insights into their tactics and intentions.

Regularly reviewing and updating firewall rules and access control lists (ACLs) is crucial for minimizing exposure to reconnaissance attempts. Security teams should adopt a least-privilege approach, ensuring that only necessary ports and services are accessible from external networks.

Education and awareness among employees are essential best practices in network reconnaissance. Phishing and social engineering attacks often serve as initial reconnaissance methods for attackers. By training employees to recognize and report suspicious emails and requests, organizations can mitigate the risk of falling victim to such tactics.

Intrusion detection and prevention systems should be tuned to recognize known reconnaissance tools and signatures. Organizations should also implement threat hunting practices, where security professionals actively seek out signs of reconnaissance activities within the network.

When detecting reconnaissance attempts, organizations should have incident response plans in place to respond effectively. Rapidly identifying and mitigating reconnaissance activities can prevent attackers from gaining valuable intelligence and reduce the likelihood of a successful breach.

Finally, organizations should collaborate with industry peers and share threat intelligence to stay informed about the latest reconnaissance tactics and evolving threats. Sharing information about observed reconnaissance activities can help the broader cybersecurity community strengthen its collective defenses.

In summary, best practices in network reconnaissance involve a multifaceted approach that combines network visibility, monitoring, access controls, segmentation, vulnerability assessments, threat intelligence, and employee awareness. By implementing these practices, organizations can proactively defend against reconnaissance attempts and enhance their overall cybersecurity resilience. Recognizing the importance of this initial phase of an attack is key to building a robust defense and safeguarding critical assets against evolving threats in the ever-changing landscape of cybersecurity.

BOOK 2

METASPLOIT MASTERCLASS

WEB APPLICATION PENETRATION TESTING ROB BOTWRIGHT

Chapter 1: Introduction to Web Application Security

Exploring the significance of web application security unveils a critical aspect of the digital landscape in the modern world. Web applications have become integral to our daily lives, powering everything from online banking and shopping to social media and healthcare portals. However, this increased reliance on web applications has also made them prime targets for cyberattacks. As a result, understanding the importance of web application security is paramount for individuals, businesses, and organizations alike.

Web applications are software programs that users interact with through web browsers. They enable us to perform a wide range of tasks, from checking email and managing finances to sharing documents and accessing online services. These applications store, process, and transmit sensitive information, making them attractive targets for cybercriminals seeking to exploit vulnerabilities for financial gain or other malicious purposes.

The consequences of a successful web application attack can be severe. Data breaches can result in the exposure of personal and financial information, leading to identity theft and financial loss for individuals. For businesses, the fallout from a data breach can include legal liabilities, reputational damage, loss of customer trust, and financial penalties.

One of the primary reasons why web application security is so crucial is the prevalence of security vulnerabilities. Web applications are complex systems with many layers, making them inherently susceptible to a wide range of security issues. Common vulnerabilities include SQL injection, cross-site scripting (XSS), cross-site request forgery (CSRF), and insecure session management, among others.

SQL injection, for example, occurs when an attacker manipulates input fields to execute arbitrary SQL commands against a database. If successful, this attack can lead to unauthorized access to, modification, or deletion of data.

Cross-site scripting (XSS) attacks involve injecting malicious scripts into web pages viewed by other users. These scripts can steal sensitive data, manipulate web content, or redirect users to malicious websites.

Cross-site request forgery (CSRF) attacks trick users into unknowingly performing actions on web applications without their consent. Attackers use forged requests to manipulate user sessions and perform actions on their behalf.

Insecure session management can result in attackers gaining unauthorized access to user accounts. Poorly implemented session management can lead to session hijacking, where attackers take over authenticated user sessions.

Web application attacks often target sensitive data, such as usernames, passwords, credit card information, and personal identification details. Protecting this data is essential to prevent financial loss, identity theft, and privacy violations.

Another critical aspect of web application security is the protection of business-critical information and intellectual property. Many organizations rely on web applications to manage their operations, store proprietary data, and facilitate communication. An attack that compromises these applications can lead to significant disruptions and financial losses.

Beyond financial and data-related consequences, web application security is essential for maintaining customer trust and brand reputation. Users expect that their data will be handled securely when interacting with web applications. A security breach can erode trust and lead to a loss of customers and revenue.

Regulatory compliance is another driver for web application security. Many industries and regions have stringent data protection regulations that require organizations to implement security measures to safeguard user data. Non-compliance can result in legal repercussions and financial penalties.

The increasing sophistication of cyberattacks underscores the importance of proactive web application security measures. Cybercriminals continually evolve their tactics, techniques, and procedures (TTPs) to exploit vulnerabilities and evade detection. Organizations must stay one step ahead by implementing robust security measures and keeping their web applications up to date.

Web application security encompasses a range of practices and technologies aimed at protecting web applications from security threats. One of the foundational principles is input validation, where user inputs are thoroughly validated and sanitized to prevent injection attacks like SQL injection and XSS.

Authentication and authorization mechanisms play a crucial role in web application security. Strong authentication practices, such as multi-factor authentication (MFA), help verify the identity of users.

Authorization controls determine who has access to specific resources and what actions they can perform.

Secure coding practices are essential for building web applications with security in mind. Developers should be trained in secure coding techniques to prevent common vulnerabilities. Regular code reviews and security testing, such as static analysis and dynamic scanning, can help identify and remediate security issues.

Web application firewalls (WAFs) are security solutions designed to protect web applications from a range of attacks, including XSS, CSRF, and SQL injection. They filter incoming traffic and block malicious requests before they reach the application.

Regular security patching and updates are critical to addressing known vulnerabilities in web applications. Organizations should stay informed about security advisories and apply patches promptly to mitigate risks.

Security testing, including vulnerability assessments and penetration testing, helps organizations identify and remediate security weaknesses in web applications. These assessments simulate real-world attacks to evaluate the application's security posture.

Security awareness training for employees is an important component of web application security. Employees should be educated about the risks of phishing, social engineering, and other attack vectors that target web application users.

Compliance with data protection regulations is a fundamental aspect of web application security. Organizations must understand their legal obligations and implement the necessary controls to protect user data.

In summary, the importance of web application security cannot be overstated. Web applications are the gateway to critical data, services, and operations for individuals and organizations. Protecting these applications is not only a matter of compliance but also a fundamental responsibility to users, customers, and stakeholders. By implementing robust security practices, organizations can reduce the risk of data breaches, financial loss, and reputational damage while maintaining trust and resilience in an increasingly digital world.

Exploring the web application attack landscape reveals the ever-evolving tactics employed by cybercriminals to exploit vulnerabilities and compromise the security of web applications. In today's digital age, web applications have become an integral part of our daily lives, from online banking and shopping to social media and productivity tools. However, their ubiquity and the sensitive data they handle make them attractive targets for attackers seeking financial gain, data theft, or disruption.

One of the most prevalent threats in the web application attack landscape is the injection attack. SQL injection (SQLi) and cross-site scripting (XSS) are two notable examples. SQL injection attacks occur when an attacker manipulates input fields to inject malicious SQL code into a web application's database query. If successful, this can lead to unauthorized access to, modification, or deletion of data.

Cross-site scripting attacks involve injecting malicious scripts into web pages viewed by other users. These scripts can steal sensitive data, manipulate web content, or redirect users to malicious websites. XSS attacks are particularly dangerous because they can affect not only individual users but also the credibility and security of the entire web application.

Another common threat is cross-site request forgery (CSRF), where attackers trick users into unknowingly performing actions on web applications without their consent. By forging requests, attackers can manipulate user sessions and perform actions on their behalf, leading to unauthorized transactions or account compromise.

Insecure session management is a vulnerability that attackers exploit to gain unauthorized access to user accounts. Poorly implemented session management can result in session hijacking, where attackers take over authenticated user sessions, allowing them to impersonate legitimate users.

Brute force attacks are another prevalent threat, where attackers attempt to gain access to web applications by systematically trying a large number of username and password combinations. These attacks are automated and can be successful if weak or default credentials are in use.

File inclusion vulnerabilities, such as remote file inclusion (RFI) and local file inclusion (LFI), enable attackers to include and execute malicious files on web servers. This can lead to unauthorized access, data disclosure, or even remote code execution on the server.

Beyond these specific threats, web application attackers often exploit vulnerabilities in authentication mechanisms, authorization controls, input validation, and session management. The attack landscape is constantly evolving as cybercriminals discover new techniques and vulnerabilities to exploit.

One notable trend in the web application attack landscape is the rise of automated attack tools and botnets. Attackers use these tools to scan the internet for vulnerable web applications and launch attacks on a massive scale. Automated attacks are capable of exploiting known vulnerabilities quickly and efficiently, making them a significant threat to web applications.

Web application attacks often have financial motivations. Attackers aim to steal sensitive information, such as credit card numbers, personal data, or login credentials, to commit fraud or sell on the dark web. Data breaches can result in significant financial losses for individuals and organizations.

In addition to financial gain, some web application attacks have political or ideological motivations. Hacktivism involves attackers compromising web applications to promote a specific cause, deface websites, or disrupt online services as a form of protest or activism.

Competitive intelligence and corporate espionage are other motivations behind web application attacks. Attackers may target business-critical applications to steal intellectual property, trade secrets, or confidential information, giving them a competitive advantage or financial gain.

The web application attack landscape is further complicated by supply chain attacks, where attackers target third-party components or libraries used in web applications. By compromising these components, attackers can infiltrate multiple web applications that rely on the same vulnerable code.

Mitigating the risks associated with the web application attack landscape requires a multi-faceted approach. One fundamental practice is secure coding, where developers build web applications with security in mind from the outset. Secure coding practices include input validation, proper authentication and authorization, and the use of security libraries and frameworks.

Regular security testing is essential to identify and remediate vulnerabilities in web applications. This includes both static analysis, which reviews the source code for vulnerabilities, and dynamic scanning, which tests the application in its running state. Penetration testing, where ethical hackers simulate real-world attacks, can also uncover security weaknesses.

Web application firewalls (WAFs) are security solutions that help protect against a wide range of attacks, including SQL injection, XSS, and CSRF. They filter incoming web traffic and block malicious requests before they reach the application.

User education and awareness training are crucial to mitigating web application attacks. Users should be educated about the risks of phishing, social engineering, and other tactics that attackers use to manipulate them into revealing sensitive information.

Regularly applying security patches and updates is essential to address known vulnerabilities in web applications and the underlying infrastructure. Organizations should stay informed about security advisories and promptly apply patches to mitigate risks.

In summary, the web application attack landscape is a dynamic and evolving threat environment. Attackers continuously adapt their tactics and exploit vulnerabilities to compromise the security of web applications. To defend against these threats, organizations must adopt a comprehensive security posture that includes secure coding practices, regular testing, the use of security tools like WAFs, user education, and timely patch management. By staying vigilant and proactive, individuals and organizations can reduce their exposure to web application attacks and protect sensitive data and assets.

Chapter 2: Web Application Reconnaissance

Exploring the process of gathering information about web applications unveils a crucial phase in the world of cybersecurity, where knowledge is power and careful reconnaissance is the key to understanding potential vulnerabilities. In the digital age, web applications have become essential tools for individuals, businesses, and organizations. These applications provide services ranging from online shopping and banking to social networking and productivity tools. However, beneath the surface of user-friendly interfaces lie complexities that require thorough exploration for security purposes.

The initial step in gathering information about web applications is often referred to as passive reconnaissance. This phase involves collecting data without directly interacting with the target application. Passive reconnaissance techniques can include searching for publicly available information using search engines, online databases, and social media platforms.

Open-source intelligence (OSINT) plays a vital role in passive reconnaissance. OSINT encompasses the collection and analysis of publicly available information from various sources, such as websites, forums, and social media profiles. Cybersecurity professionals and ethical hackers often rely on OSINT to build a comprehensive profile of a target web application and its associated infrastructure.

Domain information is a primary focus during passive reconnaissance. Gathering details about the target's domain name, registration information, and historical data can provide valuable insights into the organization behind the web application. WHOIS databases and domain registration services are commonly used to extract domain-related information.

Subdomain discovery is another critical aspect of passive reconnaissance. Subdomains are distinct sections or branches of a domain, each potentially hosting its own web application. Tools like subdomain enumeration tools can help uncover hidden subdomains associated with the target domain.

Passive reconnaissance also involves identifying the technology stack used by the web application. Determining the web server software, programming languages, content management systems, and third-party libraries can help security professionals understand the potential attack surface and known vulnerabilities associated with the technology stack.

While passive reconnaissance provides valuable insights, active reconnaissance takes the process a step further by directly interacting with the target web application. Active reconnaissance techniques involve sending requests and probes to the application to collect additional information.

One common method of active reconnaissance is web crawling or web scraping. Automated tools can systematically navigate through the web application, cataloging pages, links, and content. This process not only helps in mapping the application's structure but also identifies hidden or unlinked pages that may contain vulnerabilities.

Fingerprinting is another active reconnaissance technique used to gather information about the web application and its server. By analyzing HTTP response headers, attackers can determine the web server's type and version, along with any additional software or modules in use. This information can be crucial for identifying potential vulnerabilities and attack vectors.

Vulnerability scanning is a fundamental aspect of active reconnaissance. Vulnerability scanners, such as Nessus or OpenVAS, systematically scan the web application for known vulnerabilities, misconfigurations, and security weaknesses. These scanners automate the process of identifying common issues like outdated software, missing patches, or insecure configurations.

Beyond scanning for known vulnerabilities, active reconnaissance may also involve manual testing. Ethical hackers or security professionals manually interact with the web application to identify potential security flaws, such as input validation errors, authentication weaknesses, or insecure session management.

Information gathering during active reconnaissance should also encompass an examination of the application's functionality. Security professionals aim to understand how the application processes user inputs, handles authentication and authorization, and manages user sessions. This knowledge is vital for identifying potential attack vectors.

In addition to the technical aspects of reconnaissance, understanding the web application's business logic is crucial. This involves gaining insights into the application's purpose, user workflows, data flows, and the potential impact of security vulnerabilities on its operations and users.

Web application mapping is an integral part of reconnaissance. Security professionals create detailed maps of the application's structure, including its various pages, functionalities, and interactions. These maps help in visualizing the attack surface and planning further assessment steps.

During reconnaissance, it's essential to document all findings systematically. This documentation includes detailed notes on domain information, subdomains, technology stack, fingerprinting results, vulnerability scan reports, and any manual testing outcomes. This comprehensive documentation serves as a foundation for further assessment and helps in creating a risk profile for the web application.

In summary, gathering information about web applications is a critical phase in the cybersecurity landscape. It involves both passive and active reconnaissance techniques aimed at understanding the target application's infrastructure, technology stack, functionality, and potential vulnerabilities. The knowledge gained during this phase forms the basis for subsequent security assessments, penetration testing, and vulnerability remediation efforts. In the ever-evolving world of cybersecurity, thorough reconnaissance is essential for identifying and addressing potential threats before they can be exploited by malicious actors.

As we delve deeper into the realm of web application security, one crucial aspect emerges — identifying the entry points of a web application. Entry points are the gateways through which users and data interact with the application, making them prime targets for attackers and critical areas for security assessment. Understanding these entry points is fundamental to securing web applications and preventing potential vulnerabilities.

Web applications typically have multiple entry points, each serving a specific purpose and often associated with different levels of risk. One of the primary entry points is the user interface, where human users interact with the application. This includes web pages, forms, buttons, and other elements that users engage with to input data and receive information.

Authentication mechanisms represent another significant entry point. These are responsible for verifying the identity of users and controlling access to specific functionalities and data within the application. Weak or flawed authentication processes can lead to unauthorized access, making them a top priority for security assessment.

Web APIs (Application Programming Interfaces) serve as crucial entry points for both internal and external interactions. APIs enable communication between different components of the application and can expose data and functionalities to external services or third-party applications. Ensuring the security of APIs is essential to prevent data breaches and unauthorized access.

Input fields and data submission points within web forms are vital entry points to consider. Attackers often target these fields to inject malicious input, such as SQL injection or cross-site scripting (XSS) payloads, to manipulate the application's behavior and potentially gain unauthorized access.

File upload functionality is another entry point that requires careful scrutiny. Allowing users to upload files opens the door to various security risks, including the potential for malicious files or malware to be introduced into the application. Proper validation and security controls are essential for mitigating these risks.

Session management and cookies represent critical entry points for maintaining user sessions and state information. Insecure session management can lead to session hijacking, where attackers take control of a user's session, potentially gaining unauthorized access to sensitive data and functionalities.

Error handling mechanisms also serve as entry points where attackers can glean valuable information about the application's inner workings. Poorly handled errors may reveal sensitive details, such as stack traces or database errors, that can be leveraged by attackers to identify vulnerabilities.

In addition to the technical entry points mentioned above, it's essential to consider the human factor in web application security. Social engineering attacks, such as phishing, are entry points that target users directly. Attackers craft convincing messages or emails to trick users into revealing sensitive information or clicking on malicious links.

Identifying web application entry points requires a comprehensive approach that combines automated scanning, manual testing, and thorough analysis. Automated vulnerability scanners can help identify common entry points, such as web forms and APIs, and assess them for known vulnerabilities.

Manual testing by security professionals is essential for uncovering less obvious entry points and conducting in-depth assessments. Penetration testing involves simulating real-world attacks to identify vulnerabilities and entry points that automated tools may overlook.

Thoroughly analyzing the application's architecture and design is crucial for identifying all potential entry points. This includes reviewing code, configurations, and data flow diagrams to gain a holistic understanding of how users and data interact with the application.

Documentation and threat modeling can aid in the identification of entry points and potential vulnerabilities. Creating threat models helps security teams visualize the application's attack surface and prioritize security assessments based on the most critical entry points.

Intrusion detection and monitoring systems can play a significant role in identifying unauthorized entry points and potential security breaches. These systems continuously monitor network traffic and application behavior, alerting security teams to suspicious activities and anomalies.

Regular security assessments and vulnerability scans should be conducted to proactively identify new entry points and potential vulnerabilities as the application evolves. Security should be an ongoing process, with entry point identification and assessment integrated into the development lifecycle.

User education and awareness training are essential for mitigating the risks associated with social engineering attacks. Users should be educated about the tactics and techniques attackers use to manipulate them into revealing sensitive information or engaging in risky behavior.

In summary, identifying web application entry points is a critical aspect of web application security. These entry points serve as gateways through which users and data interact with the application, making them prime targets for attackers. Understanding the various entry points and their associated risks is fundamental to securing web applications and preventing potential vulnerabilities. It requires a holistic approach that combines automated scanning, manual testing, threat modeling, and ongoing monitoring to ensure the application remains resilient against evolving threats. In the dynamic world of web application security, staying vigilant and proactive in identifying entry points is key to maintaining a robust defense.

Chapter 3: Automated Scanning with Metasploit

Delving into the world of automated vulnerability scanning with Metasploit, we uncover a powerful tool that plays a pivotal role in identifying weaknesses within web applications and networks. Vulnerability scanning is a cornerstone of modern cybersecurity, enabling organizations to proactively assess their systems for potential vulnerabilities before malicious actors can exploit them. With Metasploit, this process is streamlined and automated, making it an indispensable asset for security professionals and ethical hackers alike.

At its core, Metasploit is a penetration testing framework that offers a vast array of tools and functionalities for assessing the security of systems and applications. One of its key features is automated vulnerability scanning, which allows users to discover and assess vulnerabilities within a target environment efficiently.

The first step in automated vulnerability scanning with Metasploit is defining the scope of the assessment. This involves selecting the target systems or applications to be scanned and specifying the scanning parameters. Users can customize the scan to suit their needs, whether it's focusing on a single web application, a network segment, or an entire infrastructure.

Metasploit's vulnerability scanning capabilities cover a wide range of targets, including web applications, network services, and operating systems. It can identify known vulnerabilities associated with common software and configurations, making it a valuable tool for assessing the security posture of diverse environments.

Once the scanning scope is defined, Metasploit employs a variety of scanning techniques to identify vulnerabilities. These techniques include port scanning, service fingerprinting, and vulnerability checks based on known exploits and vulnerabilities. The framework leverages its extensive database of vulnerabilities and exploits to identify weaknesses within the target environment.

Port scanning is the initial step in the scanning process. Metasploit uses various scanning methods, such as SYN scans and comprehensive scans, to identify open ports on target systems. Open ports are critical entry points for attackers and serve as potential indicators of vulnerabilities.

Service fingerprinting follows port scanning and involves identifying the services running on open ports. Metasploit employs techniques like banner grabbing and service version detection to determine the specific services and their versions, providing valuable information for vulnerability assessment.

The heart of automated vulnerability scanning lies in the exploitation of known vulnerabilities. Metasploit's extensive database, which includes thousands of known vulnerabilities and corresponding exploits, enables the framework to check if the target systems are susceptible to any of these exploits. Vulnerability checks can include tests for common weaknesses like SQL injection, cross-site scripting (XSS), and outdated software versions.

During the scanning process, Metasploit categorizes vulnerabilities based on severity, allowing users to prioritize remediation efforts. High-severity vulnerabilities, which have the potential to result in significant security breaches, are typically addressed first.

One of the advantages of using Metasploit for automated vulnerability scanning is its ability to generate detailed reports. These reports provide a comprehensive overview of the scanning results, including identified vulnerabilities, their severity, affected systems, and potential exploits. The reports serve as valuable documentation for security teams and stakeholders.

Metasploit's flexibility extends to scheduling automated scans to run at specified intervals, ensuring that organizations can continuously monitor their security posture and identify new vulnerabilities as they emerge. This proactive approach to vulnerability scanning helps organizations stay ahead of potential threats and reduce the risk of security breaches.

Integration with other security tools and platforms is a notable feature of Metasploit. Users can incorporate the framework into their existing security workflows, allowing for seamless collaboration with other security solutions. This integration enhances the overall security posture by leveraging Metasploit's scanning capabilities alongside other threat detection and prevention mechanisms.

While Metasploit is a powerful tool for automated vulnerability scanning, it's essential to approach scanning with caution and ethical considerations. Unauthorized or aggressive scanning can disrupt target systems and networks, potentially causing unintended consequences. Therefore, it's crucial to obtain proper authorization and adhere to ethical hacking guidelines when conducting vulnerability assessments with Metasploit.

In summary, automated vulnerability scanning with Metasploit is a valuable asset in the arsenal of cybersecurity professionals and ethical hackers. The framework's ability to identify and assess vulnerabilities within target systems and applications streamlines the security assessment process. With its extensive database of vulnerabilities and exploits, Metasploit offers a comprehensive approach to vulnerability scanning, enabling organizations to proactively address security weaknesses and reduce the risk of security breaches. As cybersecurity threats continue to evolve, tools like Metasploit play a critical role in maintaining the security and resilience of modern systems and networks.

In our exploration of web application security, we come to a pivotal stage: scanning web applications for common flaws. Web applications have become integral to our digital lives, providing us with online shopping, banking, social networking, and more. However, they are also prime targets for attackers seeking to exploit vulnerabilities and compromise user data. Scanning for common flaws is an essential part of securing these applications and protecting sensitive information.

At its core, web application scanning is a process that systematically examines a web application for known security weaknesses and vulnerabilities. It aims to identify flaws that could be exploited by attackers to gain unauthorized access, steal data, or disrupt the application's functionality.

One of the most prevalent vulnerabilities in web applications is the injection flaw. SQL injection (SQLi) and cross-site scripting (XSS) are two prime examples. SQL injection occurs when an attacker manipulates input fields to inject malicious SQL code into a web application's database query. If successful, this can lead to unauthorized access to, modification, or deletion of data.

Cross-site scripting, on the other hand, involves injecting malicious scripts into web pages viewed by other users. These scripts can steal sensitive data, manipulate web content, or redirect users to malicious websites. XSS attacks are particularly dangerous because they can affect not only individual users but also the credibility and security of the entire web application.

Another common vulnerability is cross-site request forgery (CSRF), where attackers trick users into unknowingly performing actions on web applications without their consent. By forging requests, attackers can manipulate user sessions and perform actions on their behalf, leading to unauthorized transactions or account compromise.

Insecure session management is a vulnerability that attackers exploit to gain unauthorized access to user accounts. Poorly implemented session management can result in session hijacking, where attackers take over authenticated user sessions, allowing them to impersonate legitimate users.

Brute force attacks are another prevalent threat, where attackers attempt to gain access to web applications by systematically trying a large number of username and password combinations. These attacks are automated and can be successful if weak or default credentials are in use.

File inclusion vulnerabilities, such as remote file inclusion (RFI) and local file inclusion (LFI), enable attackers to include and execute malicious files on web servers. This can lead to unauthorized access, data disclosure, or even remote code execution on the server.

Beyond these specific vulnerabilities, web application scanning also assesses the security of authentication mechanisms, authorization controls, input validation, and session management. The goal is to identify any weaknesses that could be exploited by attackers.

Scanning web applications for common flaws is a comprehensive process that involves both automated and manual techniques. Automated vulnerability scanners, such as Nessus or OpenVAS, systematically scan the application for known vulnerabilities, misconfigurations, and security weaknesses. These scanners can quickly identify issues like outdated software, missing patches, or insecure configurations.

Manual testing by security professionals is essential for uncovering vulnerabilities that automated tools may miss. Ethical hackers or security experts manually interact with the web application to identify potential security flaws, such as input validation errors, authentication weaknesses, or insecure session management.

In addition to technical vulnerabilities, web application scanning also assesses the business logic of the application. Security professionals aim to understand how the application processes user inputs, handles authentication and authorization, and manages user sessions. This knowledge is vital for identifying potential attack vectors.

Social engineering attacks, such as phishing, are another aspect of web application security that should not be overlooked. Attackers craft convincing messages or emails to trick users into revealing sensitive information or clicking on malicious links. Educating users about these tactics and raising awareness is essential for mitigating the risks associated with social engineering attacks.

Scanning web applications for common flaws also involves a proactive approach to security. Regularly applying security patches and updates is essential to address known vulnerabilities in web applications and the underlying infrastructure. Organizations should stay informed about security advisories and promptly apply patches to mitigate risks.

Web application firewalls (WAFs) are security solutions that help protect against a wide range of attacks, including SQL injection, XSS, and CSRF. They filter incoming web traffic and block malicious requests before they reach the application.

Intrusion detection and prevention systems (IDS/IPS) are another layer of defense against web application attacks. They monitor network traffic and application behavior to detect and block suspicious activities and known attack patterns.

In summary, scanning web applications for common flaws is a critical part of web application security. The process aims to identify vulnerabilities and weaknesses that could be exploited by attackers to compromise the security of web applications and steal sensitive data. It involves a combination of automated scanning, manual testing, and user education to create a robust defense against the evolving threats in the digital landscape. By staying vigilant and proactive, individuals and organizations can reduce their exposure to web application vulnerabilities and protect their data and assets.

Chapter 4: Manual Testing and Exploitation

As we continue our journey into the realm of web application security, we come across a vital aspect of the process: manual assessment techniques. While automated vulnerability scanners play a crucial role in identifying common flaws, there are subtler vulnerabilities and complex scenarios that require human expertise and a hands-on approach. Manual assessment techniques, often performed by ethical hackers and security professionals, allow for in-depth analysis and identification of vulnerabilities that automated tools may overlook.

One of the fundamental manual assessment techniques is manual penetration testing, also known as ethical hacking. In this process, skilled individuals simulate real-world attacks on web applications to identify vulnerabilities and weaknesses. Unlike automated scanners, human testers can adapt and use creative thinking to explore potential vulnerabilities and assess the overall security posture.

Cross-site scripting (XSS) is a common vulnerability that benefits from manual assessment techniques. While automated scanners can detect some forms of XSS, manual testing allows testers to craft custom payloads and explore different injection points within web pages to uncover vulnerabilities that automated tools might miss.

Another critical aspect of manual assessment is the identification of business logic flaws. These vulnerabilities relate to the application's intended functionality and can have significant security implications. Manual testers assess how the application processes user inputs, handles authentication and authorization, and manages user sessions, seeking weaknesses that automated tools cannot detect.

Authentication mechanisms are a prime focus of manual assessment. Testers examine how user authentication is implemented, looking for weaknesses in password policies, session management, and multi-factor authentication. Human testers can also attempt to bypass authentication controls using various techniques, such as brute force attacks or password guessing.

Authorization flaws, which govern what actions users are allowed to perform, are another area of concern. Manual assessment involves testing the application's authorization controls to ensure that users cannot access data or perform actions beyond their intended privileges.

Session management is a crucial element of web application security. Manual testers scrutinize how sessions are created, maintained, and terminated, as well as how session tokens are generated and protected. Session fixation, session hijacking, and session fixation attacks are examples of vulnerabilities that may be discovered through manual testing.

Input validation is a key aspect of web application security, and manual assessment techniques help identify input validation errors that could lead to various vulnerabilities, including SQL injection and cross-site scripting. Testers carefully inspect how the application handles user inputs, including data entered into forms, URL parameters, and cookies.

Insecure direct object references (IDOR) are vulnerabilities that occur when an attacker can access and manipulate objects, such as files or database records, that they should not have access to. Manual testers explore the application's access control mechanisms and attempt to access objects they are not authorized to view or modify.

File upload functionality within web applications can be a source of vulnerabilities. Manual testers assess how files are processed, stored, and executed on the server. They attempt to upload malicious files or manipulate file extensions to uncover potential security weaknesses.

During manual assessment, testers also investigate error handling and error messages displayed to users. Poorly handled errors can reveal sensitive information about the application's infrastructure or functionality, which attackers can leverage to their advantage.

Parameter tampering is a technique used in manual assessment to manipulate input values to uncover vulnerabilities. Testers modify parameters in requests to see how the application responds and whether it reveals unexpected behavior or vulnerabilities.

While manual assessment techniques are essential for uncovering complex vulnerabilities and business logic flaws, they also require careful planning and documentation. Testers must maintain detailed records of their testing activities, including the steps taken, vulnerabilities discovered, and potential exploit scenarios.

Collaboration with development teams is crucial when conducting manual assessments. Testers should communicate their findings to developers and work together to remediate vulnerabilities. This collaboration helps improve the overall security of the application and ensures that identified vulnerabilities are addressed promptly.

In summary, manual assessment techniques are a critical component of web application security. While automated scanners are valuable for identifying common vulnerabilities, manual testing allows for in-depth analysis and the discovery of complex flaws that may be missed by automated tools. Ethical hackers and security professionals play a vital role in simulating real-world attacks, identifying vulnerabilities, and collaborating with development teams to secure web applications effectively. In the ever-evolving landscape of web application security, manual assessment remains an essential tool for protecting data and ensuring the resilience of modern web applications.

Exploring the realm of web application security further, we encounter a critical phase in the process: manual exploitation methods. Once vulnerabilities are identified through techniques like manual penetration testing, ethical hackers and security professionals must go a step further to demonstrate the potential impact of these vulnerabilities and the real-world risks they pose. Manual exploitation methods involve simulating attacks to prove the existence and severity of vulnerabilities, providing actionable insights for remediation.

One of the primary goals of manual exploitation is to demonstrate the impact of identified vulnerabilities. For example, if a cross-site scripting (XSS) vulnerability is discovered, manual exploitation involves crafting a malicious payload and demonstrating how it can execute unauthorized actions or steal sensitive data within the web application.

SQL injection is another vulnerability commonly addressed through manual exploitation methods. Testers attempt to manipulate database queries by injecting malicious SQL statements to retrieve, modify, or delete data from the application's database. The goal is to show the potential consequences of the vulnerability.

With authentication and authorization flaws, manual exploitation often involves bypassing login controls or escalating privileges to access restricted areas of the application. Testers showcase how attackers could gain unauthorized access to sensitive functionalities or data.

Session management vulnerabilities, such as session fixation or session hijacking, are prime candidates for manual exploitation. Testers aim to demonstrate how an attacker could take over a legitimate user's session, potentially leading to unauthorized actions or data theft.

Insecure direct object references (IDOR) are vulnerabilities where testers attempt to manipulate object references, such as file paths or database record identifiers, to access or modify objects they should not have permission to interact with. Manual exploitation showcases the potential consequences, such as unauthorized data access or manipulation.

Parameter tampering is a technique often used in manual exploitation to manipulate input values and uncover vulnerabilities. Testers modify parameters in requests to demonstrate how attackers could manipulate the application's behavior to their advantage.

Manual exploitation also involves exploring potential attack scenarios and the chaining of vulnerabilities. Testers may combine multiple vulnerabilities to demonstrate the severity of a potential attack. For example, they might use an authentication bypass vulnerability to access an administrative interface and then exploit an XSS vulnerability to steal admin credentials.

File upload vulnerabilities, which allow users to upload files to the application, are explored through manual exploitation. Testers attempt to upload malicious files or manipulate file extensions to demonstrate how an attacker could introduce malicious code or malware into the application.

During manual exploitation, testers may also explore the application's error handling and error messages. Poorly handled errors can provide valuable information to attackers, such as stack traces or database errors. Manual exploitation demonstrates how attackers could leverage this information to identify and exploit vulnerabilities.

Collaboration with development teams is crucial during manual exploitation. Testers must work closely with developers to understand the application's architecture and potential attack vectors. This collaboration helps ensure that vulnerabilities are fully understood and can be effectively remediated.

It's important to note that manual exploitation should always be conducted ethically and with proper authorization. Unauthorized or aggressive exploitation can lead to unintended consequences and disruption of the target system or application. Ethical hackers and security professionals follow strict guidelines and obtain permission before conducting manual exploitation.

In addition to demonstrating the impact of vulnerabilities, manual exploitation methods also serve as a valuable tool for educating developers, security teams, and stakeholders. By showcasing the real-world risks associated with vulnerabilities, testers can raise awareness and prioritize remediation efforts.

While manual exploitation is a critical phase in the web application security assessment process, it is not the end of the journey. Once vulnerabilities are demonstrated, the next steps involve collaborating with development teams to remediate these vulnerabilities and strengthen the application's security posture.

In summary, manual exploitation methods play a pivotal role in web application security assessments. Ethical hackers and security professionals use these methods to demonstrate the real-world impact of identified vulnerabilities, helping organizations understand the risks they face. Through ethical and authorized exploitation, testers showcase how attackers could leverage vulnerabilities to compromise the security of web applications and steal sensitive data. This phase not only identifies weaknesses but also serves as an educational tool for raising security awareness and driving remediation efforts. In the ever-evolving landscape of web application security, manual exploitation remains a critical component of protecting data and ensuring the resilience of modern web applications.

Chapter 5: Exploiting Common Web App Vulnerabilities

Navigating the intricate landscape of web application security, we encounter a myriad of common vulnerabilities that pose significant risks to the confidentiality, integrity, and availability of both data and services. These vulnerabilities are the Achilles' heel of web applications, making them attractive targets for malicious actors seeking to exploit weaknesses for financial gain or to cause harm. To fortify our understanding of web application security, let's delve into some of the most prevalent vulnerabilities that organizations and security professionals contend with in the ongoing battle to secure digital assets.

Cross-site Scripting (XSS), a pervasive web application vulnerability, occurs when an attacker injects malicious scripts into web pages viewed by other users. These scripts execute within the user's browser, allowing the attacker to steal sensitive data, manipulate web content, or redirect users to malicious websites. It's akin to a hidden assailant infiltrating a crowded gathering, manipulating interactions from within.

SQL Injection (SQLi) is a vulnerability that arises when an attacker manipulates input fields to inject malicious SQL code into a web application's database query. If successful, SQLi can lead to unauthorized access, modification, or deletion of data stored in the database, potentially exposing sensitive information to malevolent actors.

Cross-Site Request Forgery (CSRF) is a deceptive attack where an attacker tricks a user into unknowingly performing actions on a web application without their consent. By crafting malicious requests, attackers can manipulate user sessions and perform actions on their behalf, leading to unauthorized transactions or account compromise. It's akin to a puppeteer subtly controlling the actions of their marionette.

Insecure Deserialization is a vulnerability where an attacker manipulates the deserialization process of serialized data to execute arbitrary code. This can lead to remote code execution or other malicious actions, depending on the context in which the deserialization occurs. It's as if an intruder subtly tampered with the contents of a gift box to reveal a hidden danger.

Authentication and Authorization Flaws are vulnerabilities that allow attackers to gain unauthorized access to web applications or perform actions beyond their intended privileges. Weak or poorly implemented authentication mechanisms can lead to unauthorized account access, while flawed authorization controls can permit users to perform actions they shouldn't. It's like an imposter gaining access to a secure facility or someone with limited authority exploiting a vulnerability to assume a higher role.

Security Misconfigurations are prevalent vulnerabilities stemming from improperly configured settings or insufficient security measures. These misconfigurations can expose sensitive data, grant unauthorized access, or open avenues for attackers. It's akin to leaving the front door of a building unlocked or inadvertently sharing confidential information on a public forum.

Sensitive Data Exposure occurs when web applications mishandle sensitive information, such as credit card numbers or login credentials. Attackers can exploit this vulnerability to access and misuse sensitive data, leading to financial fraud or identity theft. It's akin to a confidential document left unattended, ready for prying eyes to seize.

Insecure Direct Object References (IDOR) are vulnerabilities where an attacker can manipulate object references, such as file paths or database record identifiers, to access or modify objects they should not have permission to interact with. It's akin to a cunning infiltrator finding a way to access a secure vault.

Broken Authentication and Session Management vulnerabilities stem from flaws in how web applications handle user authentication and session management. Attackers can exploit these weaknesses to hijack user sessions or impersonate legitimate users, gaining unauthorized access or performing actions on their behalf. It's akin to a clever impersonator donning a disguise to assume someone else's identity.

XML External Entity (XXE) Injection is a vulnerability that occurs when an attacker exploits an application's XML parsing functionality to include external entities, leading to information disclosure or denial of service attacks. It's as if a trickster slipped hidden messages into a conversation, revealing sensitive information.

File Upload Vulnerabilities arise when web applications do not adequately validate and secure file uploads. Attackers can exploit these vulnerabilities to upload malicious files, potentially leading to remote code execution or the dissemination of malware. It's akin to an unscrupulous actor sneaking contraband through security checkpoints.

Security Headers play a crucial role in web application security by helping mitigate various threats. Missing or misconfigured security headers can expose applications to attacks like Cross-Site Scripting (XSS) and Clickjacking. Security headers act as sentinels guarding the fortifications of a web application.

Server-Side Request Forgery (SSRF) is a vulnerability that occurs when an attacker tricks a server into making malicious requests on its behalf, potentially leading to unauthorized data access or service disruption. It's akin to an artful manipulator persuading a gatekeeper to open doors they shouldn't.

Unvalidated Redirects and Forwards vulnerabilities exist when web applications allow users to redirect to arbitrary URLs without proper validation. Attackers can manipulate these redirects to trick users into visiting malicious sites or phishing pages. It's like a signpost that can be subtly altered to lead unsuspecting travelers astray.

While these common web application vulnerabilities may seem daunting, they can be effectively mitigated through proactive security measures, including regular security assessments, patch management, secure coding practices, and the implementation of robust security mechanisms. By understanding these vulnerabilities and the potential risks they pose, organizations and security professionals can take informed steps to protect their web applications and the data they house, fortifying their defenses against an ever-evolving landscape of threats.

As we continue our journey into the intricate world of web application security, it's essential to explore the realm of exploitation techniques for web application flaws. In previous chapters, we discussed the identification of common vulnerabilities, but understanding how attackers leverage these vulnerabilities is equally crucial.

Exploitation techniques are the methods used to take advantage of weaknesses in web applications, ultimately compromising their security.

Cross-site Scripting (XSS) is one of the most prevalent web application vulnerabilities, and its exploitation techniques vary depending on the type of XSS present. In stored XSS, attackers inject malicious scripts that are stored on the web server and served to other users, leading to the execution of these scripts within their browsers. Reflected XSS involves injecting malicious scripts into URLs or input fields, which are then executed when the victim visits the manipulated URL or interacts with the vulnerable input field.

SQL Injection (SQLi) exploitation techniques involve crafting SQL queries that manipulate the database underlying a web application. Attackers insert malicious SQL statements, often in input fields, to extract, modify, or delete data from the database. SQLi can lead to data breaches, unauthorized access, or even full control of the application's database.

Cross-Site Request Forgery (CSRF) exploits rely on tricking users into performing actions on web applications without their consent. Attackers typically create malicious web pages or emails with hidden requests that, when executed by the victim, perform actions on the target application, such as changing account settings or initiating financial transactions.

Insecure Deserialization exploitation techniques involve manipulating serialized data to execute arbitrary code within the application's context. Attackers may craft malicious payloads within serialized data to achieve remote code execution, which can lead to complete compromise of the application.

Authentication and authorization flaws are often exploited through techniques like credential stuffing, where attackers use previously leaked or stolen credentials to gain unauthorized access to user accounts. Authorization bypass techniques may involve manipulating URL parameters or exploiting logic flaws to escalate privileges or access restricted areas of the application.

Session management vulnerabilities are exploited by attackers to hijack user sessions. Techniques such as session fixation involve setting a victim's session identifier to a known value, allowing the attacker to take control of the session. Session hijacking, on the other hand, exploits weaknesses in session handling to steal active sessions.

Insecure Direct Object References (IDOR) exploitation techniques revolve around manipulating object references, such as file paths or database record identifiers. Attackers may modify parameters in requests to access or manipulate objects they should not have permission to interact with, potentially leading to unauthorized data access or modification.

Parameter tampering techniques involve altering input values in requests to manipulate the application's behavior. Attackers can modify parameters to bypass security controls, escalate privileges, or perform actions beyond their intended scope.

File upload vulnerabilities can be exploited by uploading malicious files containing executable code. Attackers may manipulate file extensions, content types, or file names to bypass security checks and gain remote code execution on the server.

Security Misconfigurations are often exploited through techniques like directory traversal, where attackers manipulate URL paths to access files or directories they shouldn't have access to. Additionally, attackers may exploit misconfigured settings to gain unauthorized access or expose sensitive information.

Sensitive Data Exposure exploitation techniques focus on uncovering ways to extract sensitive data from web applications. Attackers may utilize methods like data scraping, sniffing network traffic, or exploiting weak encryption to access confidential information.

Insecure dependencies can be exploited by attackers who target third-party libraries, frameworks, or components used in web applications. By identifying and exploiting vulnerabilities in these dependencies, attackers can compromise the security of the entire application.

Exploitation techniques are not limited to just one vulnerability; attackers often chain multiple vulnerabilities together to achieve their goals. For example, an attacker may start with a SQL injection vulnerability to gain initial access and then leverage authentication bypass techniques to escalate privileges and take control of the application.

To protect against exploitation, web developers and security professionals must understand these techniques and implement robust security measures. This includes secure coding practices, input validation, output encoding, access controls, and regular security assessments to identify and remediate vulnerabilities before they can be exploited. By staying informed and proactive, organizations can strengthen their web application defenses and thwart potential attackers' efforts.

Chapter 6: Client-Side Attacks and Web App Exploitation

As we venture further into the intricate world of web application security, it's essential to explore the realm of client-side attack vectors. While much of the attention in security discussions often focuses on server-side vulnerabilities and attacks, client-side vulnerabilities are equally critical to understand and protect against. Client-side attack vectors target the user's browser, device, or software, making them an attractive avenue for malicious actors seeking to compromise web application security.

One prevalent client-side attack vector is Cross-Site Scripting (XSS), which we explored in previous chapters. XSS attacks occur when malicious scripts are injected into web pages and executed within the victim's browser. These scripts can steal sensitive data, manipulate web content, or redirect users to malicious websites. From a user's perspective, it's like encountering an invisible trickster who meddles with their online experience.

Another client-side attack vector is Cross-Site Request Forgery (CSRF). In CSRF attacks, malicious requests are sent from a user's browser without their knowledge or consent. These requests can perform actions on web applications, potentially leading to unauthorized transactions or account compromise. It's akin to an unwitting accomplice carrying out actions on behalf of an attacker.

Malvertising, a portmanteau of "malicious" and "advertising," is a client-side attack vector that exploits online advertisements. Malicious ads may contain scripts or malware that, when loaded by a user's browser, can compromise their device or inject malware. It's like encountering a seemingly harmless billboard that conceals a hidden trap.

Phishing attacks are another client-side vector that targets users through deceptive emails, messages, or websites. Attackers craft convincing imitations of legitimate sites to trick users into revealing sensitive information such as login credentials or financial details. It's akin to receiving a forged letter that appears genuine at first glance.

Drive-by Downloads represent client-side attacks where users unknowingly download malware while visiting compromised or malicious websites. These downloads can exploit vulnerabilities in the user's device or browser to install malware silently. It's like unwittingly picking up a hitchhiker who turns out to be a threat.

Watering Hole Attacks are a sophisticated client-side vector where attackers compromise websites frequently visited by their targets. By injecting malicious code into these trusted sites, attackers can infect the devices of unsuspecting visitors. It's akin to a predator setting a trap near a watering hole to catch its prey.

Clickjacking, also known as UI redress attack or user interface (UI) abuse, involves tricking users into clicking on hidden or disguised elements on a webpage. This can lead to unintended actions or disclosure of sensitive information. It's like trying to click on one thing but inadvertently activating something else.

Man-in-the-Middle (MitM) attacks occur when an attacker intercepts communication between two parties, often without their knowledge. In client-side MitM attacks, the attacker positions themselves between the user's device and the target server, allowing them to eavesdrop or manipulate data. It's akin to someone secretly listening in on a telephone conversation.

Malicious Browser Extensions are a growing concern in client-side security. Attackers create browser extensions that appear legitimate but have hidden malicious functionalities. These extensions can steal user data, inject unwanted ads, or manipulate web content. It's like inviting a seemingly friendly guest into your home, only to discover their hidden agenda.

Ransomware attacks, which encrypt a user's files or device and demand a ransom for decryption, often start as client-side vectors. Users may inadvertently download ransomware through malicious attachments or infected downloads. It's akin to receiving an unexpected package that contains a harmful surprise.

Cryptojacking is a client-side attack where attackers use the computing power of a victim's device to mine cryptocurrency without their consent. This can slow down the device and increase energy consumption. It's akin to having an uninvited guest secretly use your computer to mine for gold.

To defend against client-side attack vectors, users and organizations must adopt a proactive security posture. Implementing security measures such as regularly updating software and browsers, using strong and unique passwords, and employing reliable antivirus and anti-malware solutions can help mitigate these risks.

User education is also paramount. Users should be trained to recognize phishing attempts, avoid suspicious websites and downloads, and exercise caution when clicking on links or opening email attachments. Additionally, the use of ad blockers and script-blocking extensions can provide an extra layer of protection against certain client-side attacks.

Organizations should employ security best practices, including web application security assessments, to identify and remediate vulnerabilities that could be exploited through client-side vectors. Implementing Content Security Policy (CSP) headers can help prevent XSS attacks, while regularly monitoring network traffic can detect potential MitM attacks.

In summary, client-side attack vectors represent a significant and evolving threat in the realm of web application security. Understanding these vectors and adopting proactive security measures is essential for both users and organizations to protect against the ever-present risks they pose. By staying vigilant and informed, individuals and businesses can navigate the digital landscape with greater confidence and security.

As we delve deeper into the fascinating realm of web application security, it becomes evident that client-side weaknesses play a pivotal role in the overall vulnerability landscape. Next, we'll explore the art of exploiting client-side weaknesses in web applications, shedding light on how attackers capitalize on these vulnerabilities to compromise user experiences, steal sensitive data, and execute malicious actions. While much attention has been rightfully given to server-side security, understanding the client-side attack surface is essential for a comprehensive defense strategy.

One of the most prevalent client-side weaknesses is Cross-Site Scripting (XSS), which we've touched upon in previous chapters. Exploiting XSS vulnerabilities allows attackers to inject malicious scripts into web pages viewed by other users. These scripts run within the victims' browsers, granting the attacker the power to steal user data, manipulate the appearance and functionality of the web page, or redirect users to nefarious websites. It's akin to a surreptitious puppeteer manipulating the strings of an unsuspecting marionette.

XSS can manifest in different forms, with stored, reflected, and DOM-based XSS being the primary categories. In stored XSS, attackers inject malicious scripts that are permanently stored on the web server and subsequently served to other users, often leading to prolonged and widespread compromise. In reflected XSS, the injected scripts are embedded in URLs or input fields and executed when the victim interacts with the manipulated content. DOM-based XSS leverages vulnerabilities in the Document Object Model (DOM) of web pages to execute scripts in a client's browser. Understanding these nuances is crucial for both attackers and defenders.

Another client-side weakness of significance is Cross-Site Request Forgery (CSRF). CSRF attacks trick users into unknowingly performing actions on web applications without their consent. Attackers craft malicious requests, often hidden within seemingly harmless links or content, which, when triggered by the victim, perform actions on their behalf within the target application. Imagine someone subtly manipulating your actions in an online world, leading you to click on links or perform actions you never intended.

Phishing attacks are a classic example of exploiting client-side weaknesses. These attacks leverage social engineering to deceive users into revealing sensitive information such as login credentials, credit card numbers, or personal details. Attackers craft convincing emails, messages, or websites that mimic trusted entities, creating an illusion of legitimacy. It's akin to a con artist wearing a disguise so convincing that you willingly share your secrets.

Drive-by Downloads are another insidious form of client-side exploitation. Malicious actors compromise legitimate websites or create malicious ones, embedding malware in the web content. When users visit these infected pages, their browsers inadvertently download and execute malware without their knowledge or consent. It's like innocently stepping into a room filled with invisible toxins.

Watering Hole Attacks represent a highly targeted client-side threat. Attackers compromise websites frequently visited by their intended victims, injecting malicious code into these trusted sources. As users navigate to these compromised sites, they unknowingly become victims, as their devices get infected or sensitive data is stolen. Think of it as setting a trap near a watering hole frequented by specific prey.

Clickjacking, also known as UI redress attack, manipulates the user interface to trick victims into clicking on concealed or disguised elements on a webpage. These actions can lead to unintended consequences, such as sharing sensitive information or executing unauthorized commands. It's akin to having your actions redirected without your awareness.

Man-in-the-Middle (MitM) attacks, though not exclusive to the client-side, can compromise user interactions with web applications. In MitM attacks, malicious actors position themselves between the user's device and the target server, intercepting and potentially modifying data exchanged between them. It's akin to having an eavesdropper secretly listening in on your telephone conversations.

Malicious Browser Extensions represent an emerging client-side threat. Attackers create browser extensions that, on the surface, appear legitimate but harbor hidden malicious functionalities. These extensions can steal user data, inject unwanted advertisements, or manipulate web content. It's like inviting a seemingly friendly guest into your home, only to discover their hidden agenda.

To defend against client-side weaknesses, both users and organizations must adopt a proactive security stance. Users should be educated about the dangers of phishing attacks, recognize suspicious websites and emails, and exercise caution when clicking on links or downloading files. Employing browser extensions that block malicious scripts and ads can provide additional protection.

Organizations, on the other hand, must implement secure coding practices to minimize the risk of XSS and CSRF vulnerabilities. Employing Content Security Policy (CSP) headers can help mitigate XSS risks, while strict input validation and access controls can thwart CSRF attacks. Regular security assessments and vulnerability scanning of web applications are essential to identify and remediate weaknesses before they can be exploited.

In summary, client-side weaknesses in web applications are a critical facet of the ever-evolving threat landscape. By understanding these vulnerabilities and exploitation techniques, both users and organizations can better protect themselves against malicious actors seeking to compromise security and privacy. Vigilance, education, and proactive security measures are the cornerstones of an effective defense against client-side threats.

Chapter 7: Web App Post-Exploitation Techniques

As we journey deeper into the realm of web application security, it's crucial to explore the concept of gaining control and persistence within web applications. While identifying vulnerabilities and exploiting them is an essential part of an attacker's strategy, maintaining that control and persistence is equally critical to achieve their malicious goals. Next, we'll delve into the techniques and tactics employed by attackers to establish and maintain control over compromised web applications.

Once attackers have successfully exploited a vulnerability, they often seek ways to maintain access to the compromised web application. One common method is the creation of backdoors, which are hidden entry points that allow attackers to re-enter the system even after remediation attempts. These backdoors can be in the form of malicious scripts or accounts with elevated privileges, providing attackers with a means to regain control if their initial access is discovered and closed.

Attackers may also employ techniques to establish a foothold within the web application. This could involve creating new user accounts, modifying existing accounts, or manipulating access controls to ensure continued access. By doing so, they increase the chances of retaining control and persistence within the system.

Maintaining control often involves evading detection mechanisms put in place by defenders. Attackers may use obfuscation techniques to hide their activities, making it harder for security teams to identify and mitigate the threat. They might encrypt or encode their communications, change file names, or use stealthy tactics to blend in with legitimate traffic.

Web shells are another tool in the attacker's arsenal for gaining control and persistence. These are scripts or small applications that are uploaded to the compromised server and provide attackers with a convenient interface to execute commands and interact with the system. Web shells can be hidden in various locations within the web application, making them challenging to detect.

Credential theft is a common method used by attackers to maintain control. If they can capture login credentials of legitimate users or administrators, they can log in undetected and continue their malicious activities. This often involves keylogging, capturing session cookies, or exploiting password vulnerabilities.

Attackers may also manipulate logs and audit trails to cover their tracks and maintain persistence. By deleting or altering log entries, they can obscure evidence of their activities, making it difficult for security teams to trace their actions. This manipulation can extend to the modification of file timestamps and access logs.

Session hijacking is another technique used to gain control and persistence within web applications. Attackers can take over legitimate user sessions, impersonating them to carry out malicious actions. This can be achieved by stealing session cookies or session identifiers, allowing attackers to maintain control without arousing suspicion.

Command and control (C2) servers play a crucial role in maintaining persistence. Attackers often establish C2 infrastructure to communicate with compromised web applications remotely. This infrastructure enables them to send instructions, receive data, and maintain control over multiple compromised systems. C2 servers are typically well-hidden to evade detection. Fileless malware is a stealthy technique employed by attackers to maintain control without leaving traces on the compromised system. This type of malware operates in memory, making it challenging to detect through traditional antivirus or forensic analysis. Fileless malware leverages legitimate system processes and scripts to carry out its malicious activities. Persistence in web applications can also involve the manipulation of scheduled tasks and automated processes. Attackers may plant malicious scripts or code within these tasks, allowing them to execute commands at specific intervals without manual intervention.

Data exfiltration techniques are essential for attackers looking to maintain control over compromised web applications. They need a way to steal sensitive information or data from the system while evading detection. This often involves encoding or encrypting stolen data and transmitting it to external servers controlled by the attacker.

To defend against attackers seeking to gain control and persistence within web applications, organizations must implement robust security measures. Regular security assessments, including penetration testing and vulnerability scanning, can help identify and remediate vulnerabilities that attackers might exploit.

Continuous monitoring and log analysis are essential for detecting unusual or suspicious activities within web applications. Security teams should be trained to recognize signs of compromise and respond promptly.

Implementing strong access controls, including proper authentication and authorization mechanisms, can limit an attacker's ability to establish persistence. This includes regularly reviewing and revoking unnecessary privileges.

Web application firewalls (WAFs) and intrusion detection systems (IDS) can help detect and prevent malicious activities within web applications. These tools can analyze traffic and behavior patterns to identify potential threats.

Furthermore, organizations should establish an incident response plan that outlines steps to take in case of a compromise. This plan should include procedures for investigating and containing the breach while preserving evidence for further analysis.

In summary, gaining control and persistence within web applications is a critical objective for attackers seeking to maintain their foothold and continue their malicious activities. Understanding the techniques employed by attackers and implementing robust security measures are essential for defending against these threats. By staying vigilant and proactive, organizations can reduce the risk of compromise and respond effectively when incidents occur. As we delve further into the intricate world of web application security, it's essential to explore the often-overlooked but highly significant topics of data exfiltration and lateral movement within web environments. While identifying and preventing vulnerabilities are crucial aspects of web application security, understanding how attackers can exfiltrate data and move laterally within an organization's web infrastructure is equally vital.

Data exfiltration, also known as data theft or data leakage, is the unauthorized transfer of sensitive information from a web environment to an external location controlled by an attacker. This could include financial records, personal data, proprietary business information, or any other valuable digital asset. Data exfiltration poses a severe threat to organizations, as it can lead to financial loss, damage to reputation, and regulatory penalties.

Attackers use various methods to exfiltrate data from web applications. One common technique is exploiting vulnerabilities to gain access to databases or files containing sensitive information. Once inside, they can download, copy, or manipulate data before sending it to their controlled servers. Think of it as a digital heist, where the attackers infiltrate a vault and make off with the treasures.

Another method of data exfiltration involves abusing legitimate functionalities within web applications. For example, attackers may misuse file upload forms to upload malicious files that contain sensitive data. Alternatively, they could manipulate export features to extract data in a structured format, making it easier to transfer externally. This technique is akin to turning a tool meant for good into a weapon.

Lateral movement is the term used to describe an attacker's ability to move horizontally across a network or web environment after gaining an initial foothold. Attackers aim to expand their influence within an organization's web infrastructure, enabling them to access additional systems, services, and data.

Lateral movement is often facilitated by exploiting weaknesses in web applications or leveraging compromised user accounts. Once inside, attackers seek ways to move laterally, hopping from one system or service to another, with the ultimate goal of accessing high-value targets.

One common method of lateral movement within web environments is credential theft. Attackers who gain access to user credentials, either through phishing attacks or credential stuffing, can use these stolen credentials to move laterally. They might escalate their privileges to access sensitive data or manipulate critical systems.

Another method of lateral movement involves abusing trust relationships within a web environment. For example, if attackers compromise a less-secure web server, they may use it as a stepping stone to access a more secure server within the same environment. This is akin to exploiting a weak link in a chain to reach a more valuable target.

Web shells, which we discussed earlier, can also facilitate lateral movement. Once attackers upload a web shell to a compromised server, they can use it as a control point to execute commands and pivot to other systems within the environment. Think of it as planting a flag on a conquered territory and using it as a base for further conquests.

Infiltrating web applications and databases often provides attackers with access to valuable data, but they need a way to exfiltrate that data without detection. To accomplish this, attackers often employ covert channels or encryption techniques to hide their actions.

Covert channels are hidden communication paths within a network or web environment that can be exploited for data exfiltration. Attackers may use seemingly innocuous protocols or channels to transfer data discreetly. This is akin to spies passing messages through secret codes or hidden signals.

Encryption is another technique used to obfuscate exfiltrated data. By encrypting the stolen information, attackers can make it challenging for security tools to detect or analyze the data in transit. It's like sealing sensitive documents in a locked box before sending them out of the organization.

To defend against data exfiltration and lateral movement in web environments, organizations must implement a multi-layered security strategy. This includes regularly patching and updating web applications and servers to fix vulnerabilities that attackers could exploit.

Network segmentation is also crucial. By dividing the network into isolated segments, organizations can limit an attacker's ability to move laterally and access sensitive systems. Access controls and user privileges should be tightly regulated to prevent unauthorized access.

Security monitoring and threat detection systems can help organizations identify suspicious activities, including data exfiltration and lateral movement. These systems analyze network traffic and user behavior to detect anomalies that may indicate a breach.

User education is essential in preventing data exfiltration through phishing attacks or social engineering. Employees should be trained to recognize phishing attempts and avoid clicking on malicious links or disclosing sensitive information.

In summary, data exfiltration and lateral movement are critical concerns in web application security. Understanding the techniques employed by attackers and implementing robust security measures are essential for defending against these threats. By staying vigilant, proactive, and informed, organizations can reduce the risk of data breaches and protect their valuable assets.

Chapter 8: Advanced Web App Security Testing

Now that we have explored the fundamentals of web application security, it's time to dive into the world of advanced testing methodologies. These approaches go beyond the basics and enable organizations to uncover more intricate vulnerabilities, strengthen their defenses, and raise their security posture to new heights.

One such advanced testing methodology is known as Threat Modeling. Threat modeling involves systematically analyzing and identifying potential security threats and vulnerabilities within a web application. This process helps security professionals understand the system's architecture, data flows, and potential attack vectors.

By identifying threats early in the development process, organizations can proactively implement security controls and mitigations. This approach is akin to fortifying the walls of a castle after carefully assessing potential entry points for attackers.

Another advanced methodology is Red Team Testing. Red teaming involves simulating real-world attacks on a web application. A red team, often consisting of external security experts, emulates the tactics and techniques of malicious hackers to test the effectiveness of an organization's security defenses.

The goal is to uncover vulnerabilities that may go undetected by traditional security testing methods. Red teaming provides a holistic view of an organization's security posture and can help identify weaknesses in processes, people, and technology. It's like conducting a full-scale war game to identify vulnerabilities in a fortress.

Continuous Security Testing is a methodology that emphasizes the importance of ongoing security assessments throughout the development and operational lifecycle of a web application. Unlike traditional security testing, which occurs at specific milestones, continuous testing integrates security checks into the development pipeline.

This approach ensures that security is not an afterthought but a fundamental part of the development process. Continuous security testing is akin to having a vigilant guardian who constantly patrols the perimeter, ready to detect and respond to threats.

Static Application Security Testing (SAST) is another advanced methodology. SAST involves analyzing the source code or binary code of a web application to identify security vulnerabilities without executing the code.

SAST tools scan the application's codebase, searching for patterns and coding practices that could lead to vulnerabilities, such as SQL injection or cross-site scripting. This approach allows organizations to catch security issues early in the development process and is akin to reviewing architectural blueprints for potential structural weaknesses.

Dynamic Application Security Testing (DAST) takes a different approach by assessing a web application while it's running. DAST tools simulate real attacks by sending malicious requests and payloads to the application, observing how it responds.

DAST can identify vulnerabilities that may not be apparent in the source code, such as configuration errors or runtime vulnerabilities. It's like a security team conducting a live fire drill to assess a building's response to emergencies.

Interactive Application Security Testing (IAST) combines elements of both SAST and DAST. IAST tools assess a web application while it's running, like DAST, but they also have access to the application's internal code, like SAST.

This dual approach allows IAST tools to provide more accurate results and reduce false positives, making it a valuable methodology for complex web applications. Think of IAST as a hybrid investigator who can examine a crime scene while also having access to forensic evidence.

Fuzz Testing, or Fuzzing, is an advanced methodology that involves sending a large volume of random or malformed data inputs to a web application to identify vulnerabilities. Fuzzing can uncover security weaknesses related to input validation and error handling, often leading to the discovery of unexpected vulnerabilities. This approach is like stress-testing a vehicle by driving it through various terrains to uncover weaknesses.

Grey Box Testing is a methodology that combines aspects of both black box and white box testing. In grey box testing, the tester has limited knowledge of the internal workings of the web application.

This approach allows testers to simulate the perspective of an attacker who possesses some information about the application's architecture but not its full source code. Grey box testing can provide a more realistic assessment of a web application's security posture. It's like solving a puzzle with some pieces missing.

Blockchain Security Testing is a specialized methodology designed to assess the security of blockchain-based applications and smart contracts.

With the increasing adoption of blockchain technology, organizations need to ensure the integrity and security of their decentralized applications. Blockchain security testing focuses on identifying vulnerabilities specific to blockchain networks, such as smart contract vulnerabilities or consensus algorithm flaws. It's akin to inspecting the unique features of a fortified vault designed to store digital assets securely.

Intrusive Testing is an advanced methodology that involves actively attempting to exploit vulnerabilities discovered during testing. While traditional testing aims to identify vulnerabilities, intrusive testing goes a step further by attempting to exploit them to determine their impact and potential risks.

This approach helps organizations understand the real-world consequences of security vulnerabilities and prioritize their remediation efforts. Intrusive testing is like a controlled fire drill that allows organizations to assess their response to a simulated crisis.

These advanced testing methodologies empower organizations to go beyond basic security assessments and adopt a proactive approach to web application security. By incorporating these approaches into their security practices, organizations can better identify vulnerabilities, respond to emerging threats, and enhance the overall security of their web applications.

Now, let's delve into the fascinating realm of targeted web application assessments. These assessments are a specialized form of security testing that focuses on specific aspects of a web application, tailored to the unique needs and goals of an organization.

Unlike comprehensive security assessments that aim to identify a wide range of vulnerabilities, targeted assessments hone in on specific areas, vulnerabilities, or functionalities. Think of it as precision surgery compared to a general check-up.

One common type of targeted assessment is a Vulnerability Assessment. In this approach, security professionals use automated tools and manual testing techniques to identify and assess specific vulnerabilities within a web application.

These assessments often focus on critical vulnerabilities such as SQL injection, cross-site scripting (XSS), or authentication issues. The goal is to identify and remediate these vulnerabilities to reduce the application's attack surface.

Penetration Testing, also known as Pen Testing, is another form of targeted assessment. Penetration testers simulate real-world attacks on a web application to assess its security defenses.

They attempt to exploit vulnerabilities, gain unauthorized access, and assess the application's ability to withstand attacks. Penetration testing provides organizations with insights into their web application's resilience against skilled adversaries.

Code Review, or Secure Code Review, is a targeted assessment that involves a thorough examination of the web application's source code.

Security professionals review the code to identify vulnerabilities, coding errors, and security weaknesses that could be exploited by attackers. Code reviews are invaluable for uncovering vulnerabilities that automated testing tools may miss.

A Web Application Firewall (WAF) Assessment focuses on evaluating the effectiveness of a WAF in protecting a web application against various attacks.

Security experts assess whether the WAF can accurately detect and block malicious traffic, including SQL injection attempts, XSS attacks, and other common web application vulnerabilities. This assessment ensures that the WAF is configured correctly and providing the intended security benefits.

Mobile Application Security Testing, often referred to as Mobile App Penetration Testing, is a targeted assessment specifically designed for mobile applications.

As mobile apps become increasingly popular, ensuring their security is paramount. These assessments assess the security of mobile apps, looking for vulnerabilities that could compromise user data or the application's functionality.

Authentication and Authorization Assessments focus on the authentication and authorization mechanisms within a web application.

Security professionals evaluate how the application handles user authentication, access controls, and privilege escalation. These assessments help ensure that only authorized users can access sensitive areas of the application.

Secure File Upload Assessment is a targeted assessment that specifically examines the security of file upload functionalities within a web application.

Attackers often target file upload features to upload malicious files that can lead to remote code execution or data breaches. Secure File Upload Assessments identify vulnerabilities in this critical area.

Session Management Assessments concentrate on the management of user sessions within a web application.

Security experts assess how the application handles session creation, maintenance, and termination. They look for weaknesses that could lead to session hijacking or unauthorized access.

API Security Assessments are tailored assessments that focus on the security of an application's APIs (Application Programming Interfaces).

APIs enable communication between different components or systems and are commonly targeted by attackers. API Security Assessments ensure that APIs are properly secured and do not expose sensitive data or functionality.

IoT Device Security Assessments are specialized assessments designed to evaluate the security of Internet of Things (IoT) devices connected to a web application.

As IoT devices become more prevalent, securing them is crucial to prevent potential security breaches. These assessments assess the security of IoT devices and their interactions with the web application.

Cloud Security Assessments concentrate on the security of web applications hosted in cloud environments. With the adoption of cloud services, ensuring the security of applications in the cloud is essential. These assessments assess the configuration of cloud resources, access controls, and data security.

Data Encryption Assessments focus on evaluating the encryption mechanisms used to protect data within a web application.

This assessment ensures that sensitive data, both in transit and at rest, is properly encrypted and follows best practices for data protection.

These targeted assessments allow organizations to prioritize their security efforts based on specific needs and potential risks. By conducting these assessments, organizations can address vulnerabilities and weaknesses in critical areas, ultimately enhancing the overall security posture of their web applications.

Chapter 9: Securing Web Applications Against Attacks

In the world of web application security, secure coding practices stand as a formidable defense against the ever-present threats that lurk in the digital landscape. These practices form the bedrock upon which secure and resilient web applications are built, ensuring that vulnerabilities are minimized, and data remains safeguarded.

At its core, secure coding revolves around the idea of writing software in a manner that mitigates potential security risks. It's akin to constructing a fortress with solid, impenetrable walls that are designed to withstand even the most determined attackers.

One fundamental aspect of secure coding is input validation. This practice involves thoroughly validating and sanitizing user inputs to prevent malicious data from entering the application. Think of it as a vigilant gatekeeper ensuring that only authorized individuals are allowed inside.

Authentication and authorization mechanisms play a pivotal role in secure coding. Authentication verifies the identity of users, while authorization defines what actions they are allowed to perform within the application. These mechanisms are like the security personnel and access control systems in a building, ensuring that only authorized personnel can enter restricted areas.

Session management is another critical aspect. Secure coding ensures that user sessions are managed securely, with strong session tokens, proper timeout settings, and robust session termination procedures. It's like ensuring that visitors in a secure facility are issued temporary access badges that expire when they leave.

Data encryption is a cornerstone of secure coding. It involves encrypting sensitive data, both at rest and in transit, using strong cryptographic algorithms. This ensures that even if an attacker gains access to the data, it remains unreadable and protected, much like locked vaults within a secure building.

Secure error handling is essential to prevent the exposure of sensitive information in error messages. Properly implemented error handling ensures that error messages do not reveal internal system details, helping attackers map out potential weaknesses.

Cross-Site Scripting (XSS) prevention is a crucial secure coding practice. It involves ensuring that user-generated content or inputs are sanitized to prevent the injection of malicious scripts. This is like guarding against saboteurs who might try to manipulate signage or messages within a secure facility.

Cross-Site Request Forgery (CSRF) protection is another vital practice. It prevents attackers from tricking users into making unauthorized actions on their behalf. CSRF protection is like having a protocol in place to verify the legitimacy of every action taken within a secure facility.

Security headers are often used in secure coding to enhance the security of web applications. Headers like Content Security Policy (CSP), Strict Transport Security (HSTS), and X-Content-Type-Options help protect against various attacks by controlling browser behavior and enforcing security policies. These headers act as additional security measures within a secure facility, ensuring that the rules are followed.

File uploads are a common attack vector, and secure coding practices include rigorous validation and handling of uploaded files. This ensures that attackers cannot upload malicious files that could compromise the application. It's like thoroughly inspecting all incoming packages to prevent harmful items from entering a secure facility.

Access control is tightly managed in secure coding to prevent unauthorized users from accessing sensitive data or functionality. Role-based access control (RBAC) and least privilege principles are often applied, ensuring that users only have access to what is necessary for their roles. This is like having a highly regulated access system in a secure facility, with different levels of clearance for different personnel.

Security patches and updates are regularly applied to keep the application's dependencies and libraries secure. Just as a secure facility would upgrade its security systems to stay ahead of new threats, software must be updated to address emerging vulnerabilities.

Code reviews and static analysis tools are essential for identifying security flaws during development. They act as security audits, ensuring that the codebase adheres to secure coding standards.

Security training and awareness programs for development teams are a cornerstone of secure coding practices. These programs educate developers about security best practices and help instill a security-first mindset. It's like training security personnel to recognize and respond to threats effectively.

Secure coding is not a one-time effort but an ongoing commitment to building and maintaining secure web applications. It's a continuous process of identifying and addressing vulnerabilities, adapting to emerging threats, and ensuring that the fortress of code remains impervious to attackers.

By integrating these secure coding practices into their development processes, organizations can significantly reduce the risk of security breaches and protect their valuable data and assets. Secure coding is not merely a technical endeavor; it's a strategic approach to building resilient web applications in an increasingly digital world.

Let's explore the world of Web Application Firewalls (WAFs) and their critical role in enhancing web application security. A WAF serves as a robust security barrier, standing between your web application and potential attackers, much like a security checkpoint at the entrance of a secure facility.

The primary objective of a WAF is to protect your web application from various threats and vulnerabilities. It does so by inspecting incoming web traffic, identifying malicious patterns and behaviors, and taking proactive measures to block or mitigate potential attacks. This is akin to security personnel diligently screening visitors and packages to ensure that no threats pass through.

One of the fundamental functions of a WAF is to filter incoming traffic for known attack patterns. It employs an extensive database of attack signatures and patterns to identify and block common threats, such as SQL injection, cross-site scripting (XSS), and cross-site request forgery (CSRF) attacks. This is similar to a security checkpoint that recognizes prohibited items based on a predefined list.

Another key feature of WAFs is the ability to enforce security policies. Security policies define the rules and actions that the WAF should take when it encounters specific types of traffic or behavior. These policies can be customized to suit the specific needs of your web application, allowing you to define what is and isn't allowed, much like setting access control rules in a secure facility.

WAFs also offer real-time monitoring and logging capabilities, providing valuable insights into the traffic hitting your web application. This monitoring allows security teams to detect and respond to threats swiftly, akin to security cameras capturing suspicious activities in a secure facility.

One essential aspect of WAF implementation is defining access control rules. These rules specify who is allowed to access your web application and under what conditions. Access control rules can be based on various factors, including IP addresses, user agents, or authentication status. It's like having a well-defined access control list that dictates who can enter different areas of a secure facility.

Rate limiting is a valuable feature provided by WAFs. It allows you to restrict the number of requests that can be made to your web application within a certain time frame. Rate limiting can help mitigate distributed denial of service (DDoS) attacks and prevent excessive resource consumption, much like controlling the flow of visitors to a secure facility.

WAFs are also equipped with capabilities to detect anomalies in web traffic. Anomalies, such as a sudden spike in requests or unusual patterns of behavior, can be indicative of an ongoing attack. The WAF can automatically flag and respond to such anomalies, similar to security personnel noticing suspicious behavior in a secure facility.

Customization is a key aspect of WAF implementation. While WAFs come with predefined security rules, they can be fine-tuned to match the specific requirements of your web application. This customization ensures that the WAF doesn't inadvertently block legitimate traffic while still providing robust protection, much like tailoring security protocols to the unique needs of a secure facility.

Regular updates and patch management are crucial for maintaining the effectiveness of a WAF. Just as security systems in a secure facility need to be kept up to date, a WAF should receive regular updates to incorporate new threat intelligence and security enhancements.

Intrusion detection and prevention systems (IDPS) are often integrated with WAFs to provide comprehensive security coverage. IDPSs can detect and respond to threats that may bypass the WAF's initial layer of defense, ensuring that your web application remains protected from a wide range of attacks, similar to having both perimeter security and internal security measures in a secure facility.

WAFs can be deployed in various modes, including reverse proxy mode and transparent mode. In reverse proxy mode, the WAF acts as an intermediary between clients and the web server, inspecting and filtering traffic before it reaches the server. In transparent mode, the WAF is placed in-line with the traffic flow but does not require changes to the application's configuration. Choosing the right deployment mode depends on your specific requirements, much like selecting the appropriate security measures for different areas within a secure facility. Regular monitoring and analysis of WAF logs are essential to ensuring that the WAF is effectively protecting your web application. Security teams should review logs for signs of suspicious activity and fine-tune security policies based on the insights gained from the logs. This ongoing monitoring is similar to security personnel conducting regular patrols and adjusting security measures in a secure facility.

Web Application Firewalls are a crucial component of modern web application security, acting as the first line of defense against a wide range of threats. Their implementation requires careful consideration of your web application's specific needs, ongoing customization, and regular maintenance to ensure optimal protection. By leveraging the capabilities of a WAF, you can significantly enhance the security posture of your web application and provide a robust defense against potential attackers, much like fortifying the defenses of a secure facility to safeguard its occupants and assets.

Chapter 10: Reporting and Remediation

Let's dive into the crucial topic of effectively reporting web application vulnerabilities—a process that plays a pivotal role in the realm of web application security. Reporting vulnerabilities is akin to sending out an alert about a security breach in a secure facility, ensuring that the appropriate authorities are informed and can take swift action.

The importance of clear and concise reporting cannot be overstated. When a security researcher, penetration tester, or concerned individual discovers a vulnerability within a web application, the details of that discovery need to be communicated effectively to the responsible parties. Think of it as conveying critical information during a security incident in a secure facility.

A well-structured vulnerability report serves multiple purposes. First and foremost, it provides the necessary information for the application's owner or developer to understand the nature and severity of the vulnerability. This understanding is crucial for prioritizing and addressing the issue effectively, similar to how a detailed incident report guides security personnel in responding to a security breach.

Clarity in reporting begins with a clear and descriptive title for the vulnerability. This title should succinctly summarize the nature of the issue, allowing the reader to quickly grasp the essence of the problem. It's akin to a concise incident headline that captures the essence of a security event in a secure facility.

Next comes the detailed description of the vulnerability. This section should provide a step-by-step account of how the vulnerability was discovered, including the specific conditions or inputs that trigger it. Much like a comprehensive incident report that outlines the sequence of events during a security breach, this description helps the reader understand the context and circumstances surrounding the vulnerability.

Accurate and unambiguous information is paramount. The report should specify the affected component or functionality within the web application, including any version numbers or configurations that are relevant. This specificity is akin to detailing the exact location or system affected by a security breach within a secure facility.

Severity assessment is a critical aspect of vulnerability reporting. It involves categorizing the vulnerability based on its potential impact and likelihood of exploitation. This assessment helps the responsible parties gauge the urgency of the issue, similar to assessing the severity of a security incident in a secure facility.

A clear proof-of-concept (PoC) or demonstration of the vulnerability is immensely valuable. A PoC demonstrates how an attacker could exploit the vulnerability, providing concrete evidence of its existence. This evidence is akin to security camera footage that captures the actions of an intruder in a secure facility.

Accompanying the PoC, it's beneficial to include details of the attack scenario. This includes information on how an attacker might leverage the vulnerability to compromise the application or data. It's like providing a detailed account of how an intruder gained access to a secure facility and what they did after entering.

Recommendations for remediation are a key part of the report. These recommendations should offer clear and actionable guidance on how to address the vulnerability. This guidance is akin to providing security personnel with a step-by-step plan to restore security measures after a breach in a secure facility.

Timeliness is crucial in vulnerability reporting. The report should be submitted as soon as the vulnerability is discovered to expedite the mitigation process, similar to immediately alerting security authorities when a breach occurs in a secure facility.

Open and respectful communication is vital throughout the reporting process. Those reporting vulnerabilities should maintain a cooperative and non-confrontational tone, recognizing that the goal is to improve the security of the web application, not assign blame. This approach is similar to a collaborative effort among security teams and personnel in a secure facility to address security incidents.

Providing contact information is essential to facilitate follow-up communication. The report should include the reporter's contact details, allowing the responsible parties to seek clarification or additional information if needed. This contact information is akin to having a direct line of communication with witnesses and security personnel during an incident in a secure facility.

Transparency and disclosure coordination should be considered. In some cases, responsible disclosure involves working with the application owner or developer to fix the vulnerability before public disclosure. This approach ensures that the issue is addressed responsibly, similar to working with authorities to resolve a security incident discreetly in a secure facility.

Once the report is submitted, it enters a process of assessment, validation, and remediation. The responsible parties review the report, confirm the vulnerability's existence, and take steps to mitigate the issue. This process mirrors the investigation and response procedures within a secure facility when addressing a security breach.

Effective reporting of web application vulnerabilities is a collaborative effort between security researchers, testers, and application owners. It's a crucial step in strengthening the security posture of web applications and protecting sensitive data from potential attackers, much like promptly responding to and resolving security incidents within a secure facility.

Exploring the realm of remediation strategies and best practices in the context of web application security is a crucial journey towards safeguarding your digital assets. Think of remediation as the process of fortifying and repairing vulnerabilities in your web application, much like reinforcing the defenses of a secure facility after a security breach.

To begin, it's essential to understand that remediation is a continuous and iterative process. Web applications are dynamic, and threats evolve over time, making ongoing vigilance and adaptation vital. This dynamic nature is similar to how security measures are adjusted in a secure facility to respond to evolving threats.

Prioritization is a key principle in remediation. Not all vulnerabilities are created equal, and it's essential to focus on addressing those that pose the most significant risk to your application. This prioritization resembles the way security teams in a secure facility allocate resources to tackle the most pressing security concerns.

Patch management is a fundamental remediation practice. Keeping all components and software dependencies of your web application up to date is essential. Just as security systems within a secure facility require regular updates to address vulnerabilities, software updates close known security gaps.

Vulnerability scanning and assessment tools play a critical role in the remediation process. These tools can help identify vulnerabilities in your web application, much like security scanners and detectors help pinpoint security weaknesses in a secure facility.

Once vulnerabilities are identified, it's crucial to establish a clear and efficient workflow for remediation. This workflow should outline the steps to be taken, assign responsibilities, and set deadlines for addressing each vulnerability. Think of it as having a well-structured incident response plan in a secure facility that guides the team's actions during a security breach.

Timely remediation is essential. Vulnerabilities should be addressed as soon as possible to minimize the window of opportunity for potential attackers. This sense of urgency is similar to the prompt response required to mitigate security breaches in a secure facility.

Communication is a key element in the remediation process. Those responsible for addressing vulnerabilities should maintain open and transparent communication with all stakeholders, similar to how security personnel in a secure facility collaborate to resolve security incidents.

Testing and validation are crucial steps in the remediation process. After applying patches or fixes, it's essential to verify that the vulnerability has been successfully mitigated and that the remediation efforts did not introduce new issues. This validation is akin to conducting thorough security testing after implementing security measures in a secure facility.

Remediation strategies should also consider the potential impact on users and functionality. Balancing security improvements with minimal disruption to users is essential. This balance is similar to ensuring that security measures in a secure facility do not impede the daily operations of its occupants.

Regular audits and assessments of your web application's security posture are essential. These audits help identify new vulnerabilities and ensure that existing remediation strategies remain effective. This continuous evaluation mirrors the ongoing security assessments conducted within a secure facility.

Security awareness and training for development and IT teams are essential components of effective remediation. Ensuring that those responsible for maintaining the web application are well-informed about security best practices is crucial. This training is similar to the ongoing security education provided to personnel in a secure facility to enhance their security awareness.

Security patches and updates should be thoroughly tested in a controlled environment before being applied to the production environment. This testing process ensures that patches do not inadvertently introduce new issues or disrupt the web application's functionality. It's similar to conducting drills and simulations in a secure facility to assess the impact of security changes.

Change management procedures should be in place to ensure that all security updates and patches are tracked and documented. This documentation helps maintain transparency and accountability in the remediation process, similar to keeping detailed records of security measures in a secure facility.

Consideration should be given to the potential need for compensating controls while vulnerabilities are being remediated. Compensating controls can help mitigate the risk associated with a vulnerability until a permanent fix is implemented. This approach is similar to implementing temporary security measures in a secure facility while permanent changes are underway.

Monitoring and incident response capabilities should be continuously refined to detect and respond to emerging threats and vulnerabilities promptly. This proactive stance mirrors the vigilant monitoring and response mechanisms in place within a secure facility.

The effectiveness of remediation efforts should be periodically assessed and adjusted based on the evolving threat landscape. Just as security measures in a secure facility are updated to address new security challenges, remediation strategies should evolve to stay ahead of emerging threats.

In summary, remediation strategies and best practices are integral to maintaining the security and integrity of web applications. By adopting a proactive and iterative approach to remediation, organizations can effectively mitigate vulnerabilities and reduce the risk of security breaches, much like continuously fortifying the defenses of a secure facility to protect its occupants and assets.

BOOK 3
METASPLOIT MASTERCLASS
WIRELESS AND IOT HACKING

ROB BOTWRIGHT

Chapter 1: Introduction to Wireless and IoT Security

In the ever-expanding realm of technology, understanding the wireless and Internet of Things (IoT) security landscape is paramount to safeguarding our connected world. Picture this landscape as a vast digital terrain filled with devices, networks, and data flows, much like a dynamic cityscape bustling with activity.

Wireless technologies have transformed the way we connect to the internet and communicate. From Wi-Fi networks in our homes to cellular networks on our smartphones, wireless connectivity has become an integral part of our daily lives. It's akin to the intricate web of roads and highways that connect various parts of a city, facilitating movement and interaction.

The IoT, on the other hand, represents the convergence of physical devices and the digital world. These IoT devices can range from smart thermostats and wearables to industrial sensors and autonomous vehicles. Think of IoT as the myriad of buildings and structures within a city, each with its unique purpose and function.

However, this interconnected landscape also brings with it a multitude of security challenges and considerations. Just as a city needs law enforcement and security measures to ensure the safety of its residents, the wireless and IoT landscape requires robust security measures to protect against potential threats.

One of the fundamental aspects of wireless and IoT security is authentication and access control. Ensuring that only authorized devices and users can connect to wireless networks or access IoT devices is crucial. It's like having secure access points and checkpoints in a city to prevent unauthorized entry.

Encryption plays a pivotal role in securing wireless and IoT communications. Much like encoding sensitive information through secure channels in a city's communication systems, encryption ensures that data transmitted between devices and networks remains confidential and tamper-proof.

Network segmentation is another essential strategy. Just as different zones in a city serve distinct purposes, segmenting networks and IoT devices helps contain potential security breaches. It limits an attacker's ability to move freely within the network.

Device security is a significant concern within the IoT landscape. Devices need to be hardened against potential attacks, just as buildings in a city are constructed to withstand natural disasters and intrusions. This includes implementing secure boot processes, regular firmware updates, and hardware-based security features.

Vulnerability management is an ongoing task in the wireless and IoT security landscape. Devices and networks need to be regularly assessed for vulnerabilities and weaknesses, much like inspecting and maintaining infrastructure in a city to prevent structural issues.

Security awareness and training are crucial for all stakeholders involved in the wireless and IoT ecosystem. Users, developers, and administrators need to understand security best practices and potential risks, similar to how residents and employees in a city are educated about safety procedures.

Physical security measures also come into play. Just as a city employs surveillance cameras and security personnel to protect public spaces, physical security for IoT devices is essential. This includes safeguards against tampering and theft.

Regulatory compliance is an ever-evolving aspect of wireless and IoT security. Just as cities have laws and regulations governing various aspects of urban life, the wireless and IoT landscape is subject to legal requirements and industry standards aimed at enhancing security and privacy.

Privacy considerations are paramount. Collecting and handling user data in wireless and IoT applications must adhere to strict privacy guidelines, much like respecting the privacy rights of individuals in a city.

Threat modeling and risk assessment are essential practices. Understanding potential threats and their impact helps organizations proactively prepare for and mitigate security risks, similar to conducting risk assessments for various scenarios in a city.

Incident response plans are crucial in the event of security breaches. Just as a city has emergency response protocols for disasters, organizations operating in the wireless and IoT landscape need well-defined procedures to address and contain security incidents.

Collaboration and information sharing within the security community are vital. Just as cities share information and resources during crises, the wireless and IoT security landscape benefits from a collective effort to identify and address emerging threats.

Security by design is a guiding principle. Just as architects and urban planners prioritize safety and security in city design, IoT device manufacturers and network providers should embed security into their products and services from the outset.

Security audits and penetration testing are ongoing activities. Regular assessments of wireless networks and IoT devices are akin to city inspections, ensuring that everything remains secure and compliant with standards.

In summary, understanding the wireless and IoT security landscape is akin to navigating the complexities of a bustling city. It requires a multifaceted approach, involving technology, policy, and awareness, to ensure the safety and security of our connected world. By addressing these challenges head-on, we can continue to embrace the benefits of wireless and IoT technologies while safeguarding against potential threats.

As we delve deeper into the realm of securing wireless and Internet of Things (IoT) devices, it becomes evident that this landscape is not without its share of challenges and complexities. Imagine these challenges as obstacles on a winding path, each demanding careful consideration and navigation.

One of the primary challenges lies in the sheer proliferation of wireless and IoT devices. Much like the rapid urbanization of a city, the growing number of devices connecting to networks poses significant security concerns. With more devices come more potential entry points for attackers.

Diversity is another hurdle. Wireless and IoT devices come in various forms, from smart thermostats and medical devices to industrial sensors and autonomous vehicles. This diversity, while fostering innovation, also presents a broad spectrum of vulnerabilities and attack surfaces.

Legacy devices add an additional layer of complexity. Just as older infrastructure in a city may lack modern security features, legacy IoT devices may not have been designed with robust security in mind. Retrofitting security onto these devices can be challenging.

Interoperability issues often arise in the IoT landscape. Devices from different manufacturers must communicate seamlessly, much like ensuring that various modes of transportation in a city can work together efficiently. This interoperability can introduce security gaps.

Resource constraints are a common challenge. Many IoT devices have limited processing power and memory, making it challenging to implement robust security measures. It's akin to trying to secure a building with limited access points and resources.

Firmware and software updates are critical for security, yet they are often neglected. Just as neglected maintenance can lead to deteriorating infrastructure in a city, failing to update device firmware and software leaves them vulnerable to known exploits.

Privacy concerns are significant, especially as IoT devices collect vast amounts of user data. Balancing the benefits of data collection with privacy rights is akin to navigating the delicate balance between surveillance and individual privacy in a city.

Security awareness among consumers and end-users is a challenge. Many people are unaware of the security risks associated with IoT devices, similar to individuals in a city who may not be fully aware of safety protocols.

Supply chain security is a growing concern. Ensuring that devices are not compromised during manufacturing and distribution is crucial, much like securing the supply chain of goods in a city to prevent tampering or counterfeiting.

Encryption and authentication can be complex to implement correctly. Ensuring that data is encrypted and that devices can reliably authenticate one another is akin to establishing secure communication channels and verifying identities in a city.

Regulatory compliance varies globally, adding layers of complexity for organizations operating across borders. Much like navigating different legal systems in various cities, organizations must adhere to a patchwork of regulations related to wireless and IoT security.

Zero-day vulnerabilities pose a constant threat. Just as unforeseen emergencies can disrupt a city's operations, zero-day vulnerabilities, which are unknown to vendors and security experts, can be exploited by attackers.

Sustainability and environmental considerations are becoming increasingly important. Balancing the need for energy-efficient devices with security measures is similar to addressing environmental concerns in urban planning.

Security fatigue can set in, leading to complacency. As individuals in a city may become accustomed to security measures and overlook potential risks, organizations can become complacent in their approach to wireless and IoT security.

Complex supply chains and dependencies make it challenging to assess and manage risk comprehensively. Similar to complex logistical networks in a city, understanding the full scope of dependencies in IoT ecosystems is a daunting task.

The dynamic nature of threats requires constant vigilance and adaptation. Just as a city must remain vigilant against evolving threats, organizations must stay informed about emerging security risks in the wireless and IoT landscape.

Resource allocation can be a challenge, especially for smaller organizations. Much like budget constraints in city planning, limited resources may limit the ability to implement robust security measures.

Human error remains a significant factor in security incidents. Just as human mistakes can lead to accidents or security breaches in a city, human errors can expose vulnerabilities in wireless and IoT systems.

The anonymity of IoT devices can be exploited for malicious purposes. Similar to anonymous activities in a city, attackers may use compromised IoT devices to launch attacks without detection.

In summary, securing wireless and IoT devices is a multifaceted endeavor marked by challenges reminiscent of navigating a complex urban environment. Addressing these challenges requires a combination of technological innovation, regulatory measures, user awareness, and ongoing vigilance. By understanding and actively addressing these obstacles, we can pave the way for a more secure and interconnected future.

Chapter 2: Wireless Network Reconnaissance

Exploring the world of reconnaissance techniques for wireless networks opens up a fascinating realm of knowledge and skills that are essential for both security professionals and those interested in understanding the intricacies of wireless communication. Much like exploring a new city, diving into this topic allows us to uncover hidden treasures and navigate complex landscapes.

At its core, wireless network reconnaissance is the process of gathering information about wireless networks, their configurations, and the devices connected to them. Think of it as an expedition to discover the layout of a city, including streets, buildings, and the people within.

One of the fundamental aspects of wireless reconnaissance is passive scanning. This technique involves listening to wireless traffic without actively transmitting data. It's akin to quietly observing the flow of people and vehicles in a city, gaining insights without drawing attention.

SSID (Service Set Identifier) enumeration is a common passive scanning method. It involves identifying the names of wireless networks broadcasting in the vicinity. This is similar to noting the names of businesses or landmarks in a city as you walk around.

Signal strength measurement is another passive technique. It allows you to gauge the distance between your device and a wireless access point, much like estimating the distance between two locations in a city based on the strength of a signal.

Active scanning, on the other hand, involves sending out probe requests to identify nearby wireless networks actively. This can be likened to asking for directions or inquiring about available services in a city by interacting with locals.

War-driving, a more advanced technique, involves driving or walking around with a mobile device to detect and map the locations of wireless networks. It's similar to exploring a city's neighborhoods to understand their layout.

Mapping the physical locations of wireless access points is a crucial aspect of reconnaissance. Just as you might create a map of a city's streets and landmarks, mapping wireless access points helps in understanding network coverage and potential vulnerabilities.

Analyzing beacon frames provides valuable information about a wireless network. These frames contain details such as the network's capabilities, supported encryption methods, and more. It's akin to reading signs and banners in a city to gather information.

Identifying hidden networks, also known as closed networks, is a challenge akin to discovering concealed places within a city. These networks don't broadcast their SSIDs, making them less visible but not entirely immune to discovery.

Stumbling upon rogue access points is like encountering unsanctioned vendors or service providers in a city. Rogue access points can be unauthorized devices connected to a network, posing security risks.

SSID fingerprinting is a technique that involves analyzing the unique characteristics of SSIDs to identify the type of device or network. This is comparable to recognizing distinct architectural styles in different parts of a city.

Passive monitoring of wireless traffic, while more advanced, provides insights into data exchanges within a network. It's akin to eavesdropping on conversations in a city to gain a deeper understanding of its social dynamics.

GPS-based mapping of wireless networks allows you to create precise maps of network coverage. This is similar to using GPS navigation to explore different areas of a city and track your movements.

Wardriving tools and software assist in automating the reconnaissance process. These tools can help identify and document wireless networks efficiently, much like using navigation apps to explore a city with ease.

Understanding the differences between 2.4 GHz and 5 GHz frequency bands is crucial. These bands, much like different radio stations in a city, offer distinct advantages and limitations for wireless communication.

Cracking WEP (Wired Equivalent Privacy) keys is a technique used to gain unauthorized access to a network, similar to attempting to pick locks in certain parts of a city. However, WEP encryption is outdated and vulnerable to attacks.

WPA (Wi-Fi Protected Access) and WPA2 encryption offer better security for wireless networks. Cracking these encryption methods is akin to attempting to break into highly secure areas of a city, requiring advanced skills and tools.

Eavesdropping on unencrypted wireless traffic is a technique used to intercept data exchanges, similar to listening in on public conversations in a city park.

Understanding the principles of signal propagation is essential for effective reconnaissance. It's akin to understanding how sound travels in different parts of a city, taking into account obstacles and interference.

Reconnaissance tools and software, similar to navigational aids in a city, provide valuable assistance in conducting wireless network reconnaissance efficiently and accurately.

The ethical considerations surrounding wireless reconnaissance are essential. Just as respecting privacy and property rights in a city is crucial, conducting reconnaissance should always adhere to ethical guidelines and legal regulations.

In summary, delving into the world of wireless network reconnaissance is like embarking on a thrilling journey through a city filled with secrets waiting to be discovered. With the right knowledge, skills, and ethical approach, you can navigate this landscape effectively, gaining valuable insights into wireless networks and their security.

Exploring the realm of identifying vulnerable wireless devices and access points is like embarking on a quest to uncover hidden treasures in the world of wireless security. In this journey, we will delve into the techniques and tools that allow us to identify these vulnerabilities, much like an explorer searching for clues in an ancient city.

One of the key methods for identifying vulnerable wireless devices and access points is active scanning. This technique involves actively probing the wireless environment to discover devices and access points that may be susceptible to exploitation. It's akin to shining a flashlight in dark corners of a city to reveal hidden objects.

SSID probing is a fundamental aspect of active scanning. This technique involves sending probe requests with specific SSIDs (Service Set Identifiers) to identify access points that respond to those requests. It's similar to calling out the names of businesses or landmarks in a city to see if they are present.

Open network detection is another critical aspect of active scanning. This involves identifying wireless networks that do not require authentication or encryption to connect. It's like finding unlocked doors or gates in a city, signifying potential vulnerabilities.

Identifying default settings is crucial. Many wireless devices and access points come with default usernames and passwords that are often unchanged by users. Discovering these defaults is akin to finding keys left under doormats in a city.

MAC address probing is a technique used to identify devices based on their MAC (Media Access Control) addresses. It's similar to recognizing individuals by their unique identification numbers in a city.

Probe requests can reveal hidden networks. These requests may contain the SSID of a hidden network, allowing it to be discovered. It's like finding a concealed passage in a city that becomes visible when someone passes through it.

Active scanning can also detect devices that respond to specific requests or protocols, such as SNMP (Simple Network Management Protocol). It's similar to identifying businesses or services in a city based on their response to inquiries.

Passive scanning complements active scanning by silently monitoring the wireless environment for vulnerabilities. This technique involves capturing and analyzing wireless traffic to identify potential weaknesses. It's like observing the activities of individuals in different parts of a city to gather information.

Identifying weak or outdated encryption protocols is essential. Some wireless devices may still use vulnerable encryption methods, much like relying on old locks that are easier to pick in certain areas of a city.

Detecting unauthorized access points, also known as rogue access points, is crucial for security. These are access points set up without permission, similar to unauthorized vendors operating in a city without permits.

Signal strength analysis can reveal the presence of hidden or distant access points. It's like using a signal detector to locate radio transmissions in a city.

Analyzing beacon frames is a valuable passive scanning technique. These frames can provide information about the capabilities and vulnerabilities of nearby access points, much like reading signs and advertisements to understand businesses in a city.

Identifying misconfigured access points is essential. These can include devices with weak security settings or devices that are not properly updated, similar to buildings in a city that require maintenance or repairs.

Vulnerability scanning tools are indispensable for identifying vulnerable devices and access points. These tools automate the scanning process, much like using advanced equipment to explore and map a city efficiently.

Understanding the differences between 2.4 GHz and 5 GHz frequency bands is crucial. These bands offer varying levels of coverage and performance, much like different transportation options in a city.

War-walking is a technique that involves walking or driving around with a portable scanning device to detect and identify wireless devices and access points. It's similar to exploring different neighborhoods in a city to understand their characteristics.

GPS-based mapping of vulnerable devices and access points allows for precise tracking and documentation of their locations. It's like creating a detailed map of businesses and landmarks in a city.

Ethical considerations are paramount in the process of identifying vulnerable wireless devices and access points. Just as respecting the privacy and property rights of individuals in a city is essential, conducting vulnerability assessments should adhere to ethical guidelines and legal regulations.

In summary, the journey to identify vulnerable wireless devices and access points is akin to embarking on an adventure through the intricate streets and alleys of wireless security. With the right knowledge, techniques, and ethical principles, we can unveil potential vulnerabilities and strengthen the security of wireless networks.

Chapter 3: Cracking Wi-Fi Passwords

Wi-Fi password cracking methods are like a set of specialized tools and techniques that allow us to unlock the doors to wireless networks, providing unauthorized access to their resources. In this exploration, we'll delve into these methods, understanding their mechanics, and discussing the ethical considerations associated with them.

One common method used for Wi-Fi password cracking is brute-force attacks. These attacks involve systematically trying every possible combination of characters until the correct password is found. It's akin to trying every key in a massive keyring to open a door.

Dictionary attacks are another approach. Instead of trying every possible combination, dictionary attacks use a predefined list of words and phrases to guess the password. It's like trying a list of commonly used keys in an attempt to open a lock.

Rainbow table attacks are more efficient than brute-force methods. They use precomputed tables of possible password hashes, making it faster to crack passwords. It's like having a reference guide to quickly identify keys based on their shape.

WPS (Wi-Fi Protected Setup) attacks target the WPS feature found in many routers. By exploiting vulnerabilities in the WPS protocol, attackers can gain access to the network. It's akin to finding a hidden entrance to a secured building.

Phishing attacks involve tricking users into revealing their Wi-Fi passwords voluntarily. This can be done through convincing emails, websites, or messages that appear legitimate. It's like persuading someone to hand over their keys by pretending to be a trusted authority.

Social engineering attacks rely on manipulating individuals to divulge their passwords unknowingly. Attackers may impersonate technical support or trusted individuals to gain access. It's akin to convincing someone to hand over their keys by pretending to be a friend.

Brute-force attacks can be accelerated using specialized tools and graphics processing units (GPUs). These tools speed up the process of trying various combinations, making them more efficient. It's like using a high-speed key-turning machine to open locks rapidly.

Cracking WEP (Wired Equivalent Privacy) keys is a technique used to gain unauthorized access to a network that still uses this outdated encryption method. It's akin to using a skeleton key to open older locks.

WPA (Wi-Fi Protected Access) and WPA2 encryption are more secure than WEP but can still be cracked using dictionary or brute-force attacks. Attackers attempt to guess the passphrase used for encryption. It's like trying different words in a passphrase lock.

Capture and replay attacks involve intercepting Wi-Fi traffic and then replaying it to gain access to the network. It's akin to recording someone unlocking a door and playing back the recording to open the door.

Eavesdropping on the handshake process between a client device and an access point can allow attackers to capture the handshake, which can then be subjected to offline cracking attempts. It's like listening to the sound of a door lock being manipulated and trying to recreate it later.

Offline attacks occur when an attacker captures encrypted data packets and attempts to crack the encryption at a later time. This can be done using rainbow tables or dictionary attacks. It's like stealing a lock and trying to pick it in a private space.

Ethical considerations are paramount when discussing Wi-Fi password cracking methods. Unauthorized access to networks and devices is illegal in many jurisdictions and can lead to severe legal consequences. Just as breaking into someone's home is a crime, attempting to break into their Wi-Fi network without permission is unlawful.

Using these methods for legitimate purposes, such as testing the security of your own network or assessing the vulnerabilities of a network with explicit consent, is essential. It's similar to hiring a locksmith to evaluate the security of your home's locks or performing security assessments within the bounds of the law.

In summary, Wi-Fi password cracking methods are powerful tools that can be used for both legitimate and malicious purposes. It's crucial to understand their mechanics, ethical considerations, and the legal implications associated with their use. As with any skill or tool, responsible and ethical use is imperative to ensure a safe and secure digital environment.

Exploring advanced techniques for breaking Wi-Fi security is like venturing into the realm of digital lock-picking, where the intricacies of encryption and vulnerability assessment play a crucial role. Next, we'll delve into these techniques, providing insights into how skilled individuals can potentially breach the security of wireless networks.

One of the more sophisticated methods is the use of advanced cracking tools that leverage the power of modern computing, such as graphics processing units (GPUs) and distributed computing clusters. These tools accelerate the password cracking process, making it significantly faster and more efficient. It's akin to having a team of experts work together to unlock a complex mechanism.

Rainbow tables, a concept mentioned earlier, are particularly relevant in advanced Wi-Fi security breaches. These tables are precomputed databases of password hashes and their corresponding plaintext values. Attackers can use rainbow tables to rapidly identify passwords based on captured hashes, significantly reducing the time required to crack them. It's similar to having a vast library of decoded keys to quickly match with locks.

Another advanced technique involves GPU-based password cracking. Graphics processing units are exceptionally suited for handling the mathematical operations involved in password cracking, making them much faster than traditional CPU-based methods. It's like having a specialized tool specifically designed for a complex lock.

FPGA (Field-Programmable Gate Array) acceleration is another approach. FPGAs are programmable hardware devices that can be customized to perform specific tasks efficiently. In Wi-Fi password cracking, FPGAs can be configured to process encryption algorithms with lightning speed. It's similar to creating a bespoke tool for a unique lock.

Brute-force attacks, while generally considered unsophisticated, can become advanced when combined with clever strategies. Attackers may employ intelligent techniques, such as generating passwords based on known patterns or using algorithms that prioritize likely password combinations. It's like employing a lockpick with intricate knowledge of the lock's inner workings.

Advanced attackers often focus on the weakest link in the security chain: human behavior. This can involve social engineering tactics to manipulate individuals into revealing their Wi-Fi passwords or security credentials. It's akin to convincing a locksmith to hand over their keyring voluntarily.

Phishing attacks, mentioned earlier, can also take on advanced forms. Attackers may craft highly convincing emails or websites that closely mimic trusted entities, making it challenging for even vigilant individuals to distinguish them from the real thing. It's like creating a replica key that is nearly indistinguishable from the original.

Zero-day vulnerabilities in Wi-Fi routers or devices can be exploited by advanced attackers. These are previously unknown security flaws that have not yet been patched by manufacturers. Exploiting such vulnerabilities allows attackers to gain unauthorized access. It's similar to discovering a secret passage into a secure area.

Targeted attacks are another advanced technique. Instead of casting a wide net, advanced attackers focus their efforts on specific individuals or organizations, tailoring their methods to the unique circumstances and vulnerabilities of their targets. It's like a skilled thief meticulously planning a heist on a valuable target.

Captive portal attacks involve creating fake Wi-Fi access points that mimic legitimate networks. When users unknowingly connect to these rogue access points, they are redirected to a captive portal that prompts them for login credentials. It's akin to setting up a decoy entrance to divert attention from the real one.

Man-in-the-middle (MitM) attacks can be advanced when executed with precision. Attackers intercept and eavesdrop on communication between a user and a Wi-Fi network, potentially capturing sensitive data or injecting malicious content. It's like a master pickpocket skillfully swiping a wallet from a distracted individual.

Advanced attackers often exploit weak or misconfigured security protocols in Wi-Fi networks. This can involve leveraging vulnerabilities in outdated encryption standards or finding weaknesses in network configurations. It's similar to finding a hidden passage in a well-fortified castle.

Legal and ethical considerations are paramount when discussing advanced techniques for breaking Wi-Fi security. Unauthorized access to networks, data theft, and other cybercrimes are illegal in many jurisdictions and can result in severe penalties. Just as breaking into a highly secure facility is a crime, attempting to breach Wi-Fi security without proper authorization is unlawful.

Penetration testing, conducted by ethical hackers with permission, is a legitimate way to assess Wi-Fi security. This process involves systematically testing network defenses and identifying vulnerabilities to help organizations strengthen their security measures. It's like hiring a team of security experts to evaluate and fortify a physical facility.

In summary, advanced techniques for breaking Wi-Fi security are both a testament to human ingenuity and a reminder of the critical importance of strong security practices. While these methods can be used for malicious purposes, they are also valuable in the hands of ethical professionals who help safeguard digital assets. Understanding the nuances of Wi-Fi security and the potential risks involved is essential for both defenders and those responsible for securing their networks.

Chapter 4: Exploiting Wireless Networks with Metasploit

Exploring the world of wireless network exploitation with Metasploit is like unlocking the secrets of digital trespassing, where understanding the terrain and utilizing the right tools can grant you unauthorized access. Next, we'll dive into the realm of Metasploit, a powerful framework for penetration testing and exploitation, and how it can be applied to wireless networks.

Metasploit, often described as the Swiss Army knife of penetration testing, is an open-source framework that provides a vast array of tools and exploits for security professionals. It's akin to having a toolbox filled with specialized instruments for breaking into different types of locks.

Wireless networks, particularly Wi-Fi, have become integral parts of our digital lives. From homes to businesses, these networks offer convenience and connectivity, but they also present opportunities for exploitation if not adequately secured. It's similar to having a heavily fortified castle with a hidden entrance waiting to be discovered.

Metasploit's extensive arsenal includes modules specifically designed for wireless network exploitation. These modules leverage known vulnerabilities and weaknesses in wireless protocols, making them powerful tools in the hands of security professionals. It's like having a set of master keys that can unlock various doors.

One of the key features of Metasploit is its flexibility and adaptability. It supports a wide range of wireless attack techniques, from capturing handshakes for offline password cracking to exploiting vulnerabilities in routers and access points. It's similar to a lockpick that can be adjusted to fit different types of locks.

Metasploit can perform a variety of wireless attacks, including deauthentication attacks, which disrupt the connectivity of devices to a network, forcing them to reconnect and potentially revealing encryption keys. It's akin to creating a diversion to distract guards while you sneak into a secure area.

Evil Twin attacks involve setting up a rogue access point with a name similar to a legitimate one, tricking users into connecting to it. Metasploit provides tools to execute such attacks, enabling unauthorized access to network traffic. It's like impersonating a guard to gain access to a restricted area.

Man-in-the-Middle (MitM) attacks, facilitated by Metasploit, intercept and eavesdrop on wireless communications between devices and networks. This can reveal sensitive information, such as login credentials or confidential data. It's similar to secretly listening in on a private conversation.

Metasploit can also exploit vulnerabilities in Wi-Fi routers and access points. For example, if a router has a known vulnerability, an attacker can use Metasploit to gain unauthorized access to the device, potentially controlling the entire network. It's akin to discovering a hidden backdoor in a secure fortress.

Wireless networks often rely on encryption protocols like WEP, WPA, and WPA2 to secure data transmission. Metasploit includes modules to crack these encryption methods, allowing attackers to decrypt network traffic. It's like deciphering a coded message to understand its contents.

Offline password cracking is a technique employed by Metasploit, where captured Wi-Fi handshakes are subjected to exhaustive password guessing. This can reveal the original network password and grant unauthorized access. It's similar to solving a complex puzzle to unlock a treasure chest.

Metasploit's post-exploitation capabilities extend to wireless networks as well. Once inside a network, an attacker can use Metasploit to pivot, compromising other devices or segments of the network. It's akin to moving stealthily through a series of interconnected chambers.

Ethical considerations are paramount when using Metasploit for wireless network exploitation. Unauthorized access to networks, data theft, and other cybercrimes are illegal in many jurisdictions and can result in severe penalties. Just as breaking into a secure facility is a crime, attempting to breach Wi-Fi security without proper authorization is unlawful.

Penetration testing, conducted by ethical hackers with explicit permission, is a legitimate way to assess the security of wireless networks. These professionals use Metasploit and similar tools to identify vulnerabilities and help organizations fortify their defenses. It's like hiring a team of security experts to evaluate and enhance the protection of a physical fortress.

In summary, leveraging Metasploit for wireless network exploitation is a powerful yet double-edged sword. While it can be used for malicious purposes, it also serves as a vital tool in the arsenal of ethical hackers and security professionals dedicated to protecting digital assets. Understanding its capabilities and the ethical boundaries is essential for those responsible for securing wireless networks and defending against potential threats. Exploring the topic of gaining unauthorized access to wireless resources is like delving into the shadowy world of digital trespassing, where individuals with ill intentions seek entry into networks and devices without permission. Next, we'll discuss the various methods and techniques employed by attackers to breach the security of wireless resources. Wireless resources, including Wi-Fi networks and Bluetooth devices, have become ubiquitous in our daily lives, offering convenience and connectivity. However, they also present enticing targets for unauthorized access. It's akin to having a secure vault with multiple layers of protection, waiting for a cunning thief to find a vulnerability. One of the most common methods used to gain unauthorized access to wireless resources is password cracking. Attackers employ various techniques to guess or crack the passwords protecting Wi-Fi networks, Bluetooth devices, or other wireless systems. It's similar to attempting to decipher the combination to a locked safe. For Wi-Fi networks, attackers often utilize dictionary attacks, where they try a long list of potential passwords, such as common words or phrases. These attacks are like systematically testing different keys to see which one unlocks the door.

Brute-force attacks, another method, involve trying every possible combination of characters until the correct password is discovered. It's akin to a relentless burglar trying every conceivable key in a lock.

Rainbow tables are precomputed databases that contain password hashes and their corresponding plaintext values. Attackers can use these tables to rapidly identify passwords based on captured hashes, significantly reducing the time required to crack them. It's like having a vast library of decoded keys to quickly match with locks.

Wi-Fi handshakes, which occur when a device connects to a network, can be captured by attackers and used for offline password cracking. It's similar to eavesdropping on a conversation and then analyzing it later to understand its contents.

Evil Twin attacks involve setting up a rogue access point with a name similar to a legitimate one, tricking users into connecting to it. Attackers can then intercept traffic and potentially gain access to sensitive information. It's akin to creating a decoy entrance to divert attention from the real one.

Phishing attacks target individuals by tricking them into revealing their Wi-Fi network passwords. Attackers may send convincing emails or create fake login portals that appear legitimate. It's similar to a con artist using deception to gain access to a secure facility. Man-in-the-Middle (MitM) attacks are employed to intercept and eavesdrop on wireless communications between devices and networks. Attackers can capture data transmitted between users and wireless resources, potentially gaining access to sensitive information. It's like secretly listening in on a private conversation.

Zero-day vulnerabilities, which are previously unknown security flaws, can be exploited by attackers to gain unauthorized access. If a wireless device or network has a hidden vulnerability, it can be exploited for malicious purposes. It's similar to discovering a hidden passage into a secure area. Captive portal attacks involve creating fake login pages that mimic legitimate Wi-Fi login screens. When users connect to a rogue access point, they are prompted to enter their credentials, which attackers can then capture. It's akin to setting up a fake reception desk to gather information from unsuspecting visitors. Bluetooth devices are also susceptible to unauthorized access. Attackers can use specialized tools to identify and connect to vulnerable Bluetooth devices, potentially gaining control over them. It's like a thief picking a digital lock to gain entry. Legal and ethical considerations are essential when discussing gaining unauthorized access to wireless resources. Unauthorized access, data theft, and other cybercrimes are illegal in many jurisdictions and can result in severe penalties. Just as breaking into a secure physical facility is a crime, attempting to breach wireless security without proper authorization is unlawful.

Penetration testing, conducted by ethical hackers with explicit permission, is a legitimate way to assess the security of wireless resources. These professionals use various techniques to identify vulnerabilities and help organizations strengthen their security measures. It's like hiring a team of security experts to evaluate and fortify a physical fortress.

In summary, gaining unauthorized access to wireless resources is a topic that underscores the importance of robust security practices and ethical considerations in the digital age. While these methods can be used for malicious purposes, they also serve as a reminder of the critical need for strong authentication and encryption to protect wireless networks and devices from potential threats. Understanding the risks and ethical boundaries is essential for both defenders and those responsible for securing wireless resources.

Chapter 5: Bluetooth and IoT Device Vulnerabilities

Let's delve into the realm of Bluetooth technology and explore the vulnerabilities that can potentially compromise the security and privacy of our connected devices. Bluetooth, with its convenience and versatility, has become an integral part of our daily lives, enabling wireless communication between smartphones, tablets, headphones, and countless other devices. However, like any technology, it is not immune to vulnerabilities and security risks.

At its core, Bluetooth is a wireless communication protocol designed for short-range connections. It operates on the 2.4 GHz ISM (Industrial, Scientific, and Medical) band, making it susceptible to interference from other devices operating in the same frequency range. This interference can disrupt Bluetooth connections, leading to connectivity issues and potential vulnerabilities. Imagine a crowded room where multiple conversations are happening simultaneously, making it challenging to maintain a private discussion.

One of the primary concerns in Bluetooth security is device pairing. When two Bluetooth-enabled devices pair, they establish a trusted connection, and often this process involves a PIN or passkey for authentication. However, weak or easily guessable PINs can pose a significant security risk. It's similar to using a simple combination lock on a high-security vault – it might be easy for an attacker to guess the code.

Bluetooth devices can also be vulnerable to eavesdropping. Since Bluetooth operates over radio waves, an attacker within the range of the Bluetooth signal can intercept and capture data transmitted between devices. This could include sensitive information like phone calls, text messages, or files being shared. Think of it as someone nearby listening in on your phone conversation without your knowledge.

Another potential security risk in Bluetooth technology is the use of outdated or unpatched Bluetooth stacks and software. Manufacturers may not always provide timely updates and security patches for their Bluetooth-enabled devices, leaving them vulnerable to known exploits and attacks. It's akin to using an old and outdated lock on your front door that burglars have learned to pick easily.

Bluetooth connections can also be susceptible to man-in-the-middle (MitM) attacks. In a MitM attack, an attacker intercepts and possibly alters the communication between two Bluetooth devices without their knowledge. This could lead to data manipulation or the introduction of malicious content into the communication stream. Imagine a scenario where someone secretly relays messages between you and a friend, altering the content along the way.

Some Bluetooth vulnerabilities stem from the way devices handle pairing requests. In some cases, devices may not properly authenticate or encrypt their connections during the pairing process, leaving them open to potential exploitation. It's similar to a security guard at a gated entrance failing to verify the identity of visitors.

The Bluetooth protocol itself has undergone various iterations and updates over the years to enhance security. However, older Bluetooth versions, such as Bluetooth 4.0 and earlier, may have more vulnerabilities than their newer counterparts. Devices using these older versions are at a higher risk of being targeted by attackers. It's like using an outdated security system in your home that doesn't provide the same level of protection as modern technology.

Bluetooth beacons, which are devices that broadcast signals to nearby smartphones and other devices, can also pose security and privacy risks. Malicious actors can set up rogue Bluetooth beacons to track the movements and activities of individuals without their consent. Think of it as someone secretly following you and recording your actions.

Bluetooth attacks can also target specific device vulnerabilities. For example, some Bluetooth-enabled smart locks and IoT devices may have weak security measures, making them easier targets for attackers looking to gain unauthorized access. It's akin to a burglar identifying a poorly secured window as their point of entry.

While we've discussed several vulnerabilities in Bluetooth technology, it's essential to emphasize that manufacturers and security experts continuously work to address these issues. Newer Bluetooth versions, like Bluetooth 5.0 and 5.1, have introduced security enhancements, including improved encryption and authentication methods.

To mitigate Bluetooth vulnerabilities, users can take several steps, such as keeping their devices and software up to date, using strong and unique PINs or passkeys for pairing, and being cautious when connecting to unfamiliar Bluetooth devices or networks. These practices are akin to locking your doors, installing a security system, and being cautious when encountering unfamiliar individuals.

In summary, while Bluetooth technology offers remarkable convenience and connectivity, it is not without its vulnerabilities. Understanding these vulnerabilities and taking proactive measures to secure Bluetooth-enabled devices is crucial in today's interconnected world. As technology continues to evolve, so too will the security measures designed to protect our wireless connections.

As we embark on the journey of understanding the fascinating world of the Internet of Things (IoT), it's important to shed light on the security concerns that accompany these interconnected devices. IoT has ushered in an era where everyday objects, from thermostats and refrigerators to cars and wearable devices, are imbued with digital intelligence and connected to the internet.

The convenience and automation that IoT devices offer have undoubtedly enhanced our lives, but they also introduce a plethora of security challenges that require our attention. Imagine a world where your coffee maker can communicate with your alarm clock to ensure you wake up to a freshly brewed cup, but also imagine the implications if someone else gains control of these devices.

One of the fundamental concerns with IoT devices is their sheer volume and diversity. With billions of IoT devices in circulation, each with varying levels of security, the attack surface for potential threats expands exponentially. Think of it as guarding an enormous and ever-expanding city with countless entry points and vulnerabilities.

IoT devices are often designed with a primary focus on functionality and cost-effectiveness, sometimes relegating security to a secondary consideration. Manufacturers may rush to bring products to market, leaving vulnerabilities unaddressed. It's akin to constructing a beautiful building without reinforcing its foundation.

Many IoT devices lack the capability for regular software updates and security patches. This means that once a vulnerability is discovered, it can persist indefinitely, leaving devices exposed to exploitation. It's like owning a car that can never receive recall fixes for safety issues.

Inadequate authentication and authorization mechanisms are another prevalent concern. Some IoT devices may rely on default usernames and passwords that are rarely changed, making them vulnerable to brute-force attacks. Imagine leaving your front door unlocked with a key under the doormat.

IoT devices often communicate through wireless networks, which can be susceptible to eavesdropping and interception by attackers. This can lead to the exposure of sensitive data, such as personal information or device control commands. It's similar to someone intercepting your private conversations over the airwaves.

The sheer diversity of IoT protocols and communication standards can create confusion and complexity. Compatibility issues between devices and networks may lead to security vulnerabilities as devices attempt to communicate in less secure ways. Think of it as trying to have a conversation with someone who speaks a different language.

Privacy concerns also loom large in the IoT landscape. Some IoT devices collect extensive data about user behavior and preferences, raising questions about how that data is stored, shared, and protected. It's akin to having someone constantly monitor your activities and preferences without your consent.

IoT devices are not immune to malware and botnet attacks. Compromised IoT devices can be harnessed by cybercriminals to carry out large-scale attacks, such as Distributed Denial of Service (DDoS) attacks. Imagine a scenario where your smart thermostat becomes a pawn in a massive cyberattack.

Physical security of IoT devices is often overlooked. Attackers may gain access to devices through physical means, such as stealing them or tampering with them in unsecured environments. It's like someone breaking into your home to tamper with your appliances.

Supply chain vulnerabilities can also impact the security of IoT devices. Malicious actors may exploit weaknesses in the supply chain to compromise devices before they even reach the end user. Think of it as someone tampering with a product before it reaches the store shelves.

Regulatory challenges and the lack of standardized security practices further compound IoT security concerns. With no universally accepted set of security standards, manufacturers may struggle to implement consistent security measures. It's akin to navigating a complex maze with ever-changing rules.

As we navigate these security concerns, it's important to recognize that many stakeholders play a role in addressing IoT security challenges. Manufacturers must prioritize security in their device designs, offering regular updates and robust authentication mechanisms. Users must also take proactive steps to secure their IoT devices, including changing default passwords and keeping firmware up to date.

Government agencies and industry organizations can contribute by establishing security standards and regulations that incentivize manufacturers to adhere to best practices. Security researchers play a critical role in identifying vulnerabilities and helping to improve the overall security posture of IoT devices.

In summary, the world of IoT offers immense promise and convenience, but it also raises significant security concerns that demand our attention and collective effort. As we embrace the benefits of a more connected world, it is our responsibility to safeguard our digital realm, ensuring that the devices we rely on are not unwitting accomplices in the schemes of cybercriminals.

Chapter 6: Hacking Bluetooth Devices

In the ever-evolving landscape of technology, Bluetooth hacking techniques have emerged as a topic of significant interest and concern. Bluetooth, once seen as a convenient wireless technology for connecting devices, has also become a potential target for cyberattacks and exploitation. Let's embark on a journey to explore the world of Bluetooth hacking and understand the techniques that can be employed by both malicious actors and ethical hackers.

Bluetooth technology has permeated our daily lives, enabling us to connect our smartphones, headphones, speakers, and a multitude of other devices seamlessly. However, with this convenience comes vulnerability, as the very features that make Bluetooth accessible and user-friendly can also be exploited by those with malicious intent. Think of it as the convenience of having your favorite music play on your wireless headphones versus the possibility of someone intercepting your audio stream.

One of the most basic Bluetooth hacking techniques is known as "Bluejacking." This technique involves sending unsolicited messages or vCards to nearby Bluetooth-enabled devices. While not inherently malicious, it can be used to annoy or harass users by sending unwanted content. Imagine receiving an unexpected message on your smartphone from an unknown sender.

"Bluesnarfing" is another technique that goes a step further, allowing attackers to access and steal data from a Bluetooth-enabled device without the user's consent. This can include contacts, text messages, or even calendar entries. It's like someone secretly accessing your personal notebook and copying your contacts.

A more advanced Bluetooth hacking technique is "Bluebugging." This method allows an attacker to take control of a Bluetooth-enabled device and use it to make calls, send messages, or perform other actions without the device owner's knowledge or consent. Think of it as someone hijacking your smartphone and using it as their own.

Bluetooth vulnerabilities, such as weak or default PINs, can be exploited through a technique known as "Brute Force." Attackers systematically try different PIN combinations until they gain access to a device. This is akin to a burglar trying various keys until they find one that unlocks your front door.

"Man-in-the-Middle" (MitM) attacks can also target Bluetooth connections. In a MitM attack, the attacker intercepts and possibly alters the communication between two Bluetooth devices without their knowledge. This can lead to data manipulation or the introduction of malicious content into the communication stream. It's like someone secretly relaying messages between you and a friend, altering the content along the way.

Bluetooth devices may not always implement proper authentication and encryption measures during the pairing process. This vulnerability can be exploited through a technique called "Bluetooth Sniffing." Attackers can intercept and eavesdrop on the data being exchanged between devices. It's akin to someone listening in on your private conversation without your knowledge.

A particularly insidious Bluetooth hacking technique is the deployment of rogue devices or "Bluetooth Honeypots."

These malicious devices mimic legitimate Bluetooth peripherals, such as keyboards or mice, to gain unauthorized access to a user's device. Think of it as a baited trap set to capture unwitting victims.

Attackers may also target the "Bluetooth Stack," which is the software responsible for managing Bluetooth connections on a device. Vulnerabilities in the stack can be exploited to execute arbitrary code or gain control over the device. It's like finding a hidden vulnerability in the foundation of a building that allows an attacker to take control.

"Bluetooth Denial of Service" (DoS) attacks can disrupt the normal operation of Bluetooth devices by flooding them with connection requests or malicious data packets. This can render devices temporarily or permanently unusable. Imagine a traffic jam where vehicles block the road, preventing others from passing through.

The proliferation of Bluetooth Low Energy (BLE) devices, such as fitness trackers and smart locks, has introduced new security considerations. These devices often use weak security measures and may transmit data that is susceptible to interception. It's like using a low-security lock on a door that protects valuable possessions.

Ethical hackers and security researchers play a crucial role in identifying and mitigating Bluetooth vulnerabilities. By responsibly disclosing vulnerabilities to manufacturers and working to improve security measures, they contribute to a safer Bluetooth ecosystem. Think of them as digital guardians who protect the realm of wireless connectivity.

In summary, Bluetooth hacking techniques have become a part of the cybersecurity landscape, highlighting the need for vigilance and security awareness when using

Bluetooth-enabled devices. While the convenience of wireless connectivity is undeniable, it is essential to understand the potential risks and take steps to protect our devices and data. As technology evolves, so too must our commitment to securing the digital world we inhabit.

In the realm of cybersecurity, the unauthorized access and control of Bluetooth devices have become increasingly prevalent concerns in today's interconnected world. Imagine a scenario where your Bluetooth-enabled headphones suddenly start playing music you didn't choose, or your smartphone begins sending text messages without your consent. These situations might sound like something out of a science fiction movie, but they are very real threats in the digital landscape.

One of the fundamental challenges in the world of Bluetooth security is the inherent convenience of the technology itself. Bluetooth was designed to make our lives easier by enabling wireless connections between devices. Whether it's your smartphone connecting to your wireless earbuds or your laptop syncing with your wireless keyboard, Bluetooth offers seamless connectivity. However, this convenience can also be a double-edged sword, as it creates opportunities for malicious actors to exploit vulnerabilities.

One common technique employed by malicious hackers is known as "Bluejacking." This tactic involves sending unsolicited messages or vCards to nearby Bluetooth-enabled devices. While Bluejacking may not inherently harm your device, it can be an annoying intrusion into your digital space. Imagine receiving a mysterious message on your smartphone from an unknown sender, disrupting your peaceful digital experience.

Taking a step further, we encounter the technique of "Bluesnarfing." In a Bluesnarfing attack, cybercriminals gain unauthorized access to your Bluetooth-enabled device and steal sensitive data without your knowledge or consent. This data could include your contacts, text messages, or even your calendar entries. It's akin to someone secretly accessing your personal notebook and copying your private information without your permission.

The most advanced level of Bluetooth hacking is "Bluebugging." In a Bluebugging attack, attackers not only gain unauthorized access to your Bluetooth-enabled device but also assume control over it. This means they can make calls, send messages, or perform other actions using your device without you having any inkling of what's happening. Picture someone hijacking your smartphone and using it as if it were their own.

To execute these Bluetooth attacks, malicious actors often exploit vulnerabilities in Bluetooth security protocols. One such vulnerability is weak or default Personal Identification Numbers (PINs) and passwords. Attackers can employ a technique known as "Brute Force" to systematically try different PIN combinations until they gain access to the target device. It's similar to a thief attempting various keys until they find the one that unlocks your front door.

Another avenue of attack is through "Man-in-the-Middle" (MitM) attacks. In a MitM attack, the attacker intercepts and possibly alters the communication between two Bluetooth devices without their knowledge. This can lead to data manipulation or the introduction of malicious content into the communication stream. It's as if someone intercepted your mail and tampered with its contents before delivering it to you.

Bluetooth eavesdropping is another concerning technique. When devices don't implement proper authentication and encryption during the pairing process, attackers can intercept and listen in on the data being exchanged between the devices. It's akin to someone listening in on your private conversation without your consent, potentially gaining access to sensitive information.

Deploying rogue devices, often referred to as "Bluetooth Honeypots," is a particularly insidious tactic. These malicious devices mimic legitimate Bluetooth peripherals, such as keyboards or mice, to gain unauthorized access to a user's device. Imagine a deceptive trap set to capture unsuspecting victims who unwittingly connect to the rogue device, exposing their data and device to potential compromise.

Attackers may also target vulnerabilities in the "Bluetooth Stack," which is the software responsible for managing Bluetooth connections on a device. Exploiting weaknesses in the stack can allow attackers to execute arbitrary code or gain control over the device. It's like finding a hidden vulnerability in the foundation of a building, giving an attacker access to the entire structure.

Furthermore, "Bluetooth Denial of Service" (DoS) attacks can disrupt the normal operation of Bluetooth devices. Attackers flood the devices with connection requests or malicious data packets, rendering them temporarily or permanently unusable. Think of it as a deliberate traffic jam where vehicles block the road, preventing others from passing through.

As Bluetooth technology continues to evolve, so do the techniques employed by malicious actors. The proliferation of Bluetooth Low Energy (BLE) devices, including fitness trackers and smart locks, has introduced new security considerations. These devices often use weaker security measures and may transmit data susceptible to interception. It's like using a low-security lock to protect valuable possessions.

In light of these security concerns, ethical hackers and security researchers play a crucial role in identifying and mitigating Bluetooth vulnerabilities. By responsibly disclosing vulnerabilities to manufacturers and collaborating to improve security measures, they contribute to a safer Bluetooth ecosystem. Think of them as digital guardians who protect the realm of wireless connectivity, ensuring that Bluetooth technology remains convenient and secure.

In summary, unauthorized access and control of Bluetooth devices pose real and significant threats in our increasingly interconnected world. While Bluetooth technology offers undeniable convenience, it is essential to understand and address the potential risks it carries. As technology evolves, so must our commitment to securing the digital world we inhabit.

Chapter 7: IoT Device Exploitation with Metasploit

Exploring the vast world of IoT, we find an ecosystem filled with interconnected devices, ranging from smart thermostats to internet-connected refrigerators. These devices have undoubtedly made our lives more convenient, but they also introduce a new frontier for cybersecurity concerns. Next, we'll delve into the intriguing realm of Metasploit for IoT device exploitation, understanding how this powerful tool can be harnessed for both ethical hacking and security enhancement.

IoT devices, by design, collect and transmit data to improve our daily experiences. However, their ubiquitous presence and often lax security measures have made them appealing targets for malicious actors. Vulnerabilities in these devices can lead to privacy breaches, data theft, and even the potential compromise of critical infrastructure.

Metasploit, a well-known penetration testing framework, has evolved to address the unique challenges presented by IoT security. It equips cybersecurity professionals with a potent arsenal for assessing and securing these smart devices. Metasploit's modular architecture, vast collection of exploits, and user-friendly interface make it an invaluable tool for both ethical hackers and security experts.

One of the fundamental steps in IoT device exploitation is reconnaissance. This involves gathering information about the target device, such as its firmware version, communication protocols, and potential vulnerabilities. Metasploit simplifies this process by providing various modules designed to identify and fingerprint IoT devices automatically.

Once the reconnaissance phase is complete, the next step is vulnerability assessment. Metasploit offers a range of exploits and payloads that can be leveraged to test the security of IoT devices. These exploits are carefully crafted to target known vulnerabilities, providing cybersecurity professionals with a means to assess the device's susceptibility to attacks.

IoT device exploitation often involves gaining unauthorized access to the device, and Metasploit excels in this area. It provides modules for brute-force attacks, enabling testers to crack weak passwords and gain entry. Additionally, Metasploit offers a comprehensive set of post-exploitation modules that allow for maintaining access to compromised devices.

One of the key challenges in IoT security is the diversity of devices and their underlying architectures. Metasploit's versatility shines here, as it supports a wide array of hardware and software platforms commonly found in IoT ecosystems. This adaptability allows security professionals to assess the security of IoT devices across various manufacturers and product lines.

IoT devices frequently rely on wireless communication protocols like Zigbee or Z-Wave. Metasploit is well-equipped to handle these protocols, offering modules that facilitate the exploitation of wireless vulnerabilities. These modules can help testers identify and assess the security of IoT devices operating on these protocols.

Bluetooth Low Energy (BLE) is another commonly used communication standard in IoT devices. Metasploit's BLE modules enable security experts to assess the security of

BLE-enabled devices, from smart locks to fitness trackers. This capability is crucial in identifying and mitigating potential threats in the ever-expanding world of IoT.

In addition to individual device assessments, Metasploit is valuable for evaluating the security of entire IoT ecosystems. Security researchers can use it to simulate large-scale attacks on IoT networks, providing insights into vulnerabilities that may be exploited by malicious actors seeking to compromise multiple devices.

Metasploit's extensive exploit database is continually updated, ensuring that security professionals have access to the latest vulnerabilities and exploits for IoT devices. This dynamic nature enables testers to stay one step ahead of potential threats and helps manufacturers identify and address security flaws promptly.

While Metasploit is a powerful tool for IoT device exploitation, it is essential to approach its usage with ethical considerations in mind. Testing IoT devices without proper authorization is illegal and unethical. Therefore, ethical hackers and security experts must obtain explicit consent from device owners or manufacturers before conducting assessments.

In summary, Metasploit plays a pivotal role in IoT security by providing cybersecurity professionals with the tools needed to assess and enhance the security of IoT devices. Its adaptability, vast exploit database, and user-friendly interface make it an invaluable asset in the ongoing battle to protect the interconnected world of IoT. With responsible usage, Metasploit can help secure IoT ecosystems, ensuring that the convenience of smart devices does not come at the cost of security and privacy.

As we venture further into the realm of IoT security, one critical aspect that demands our attention is gaining control over IoT devices. This chapter will explore the intricacies of asserting control over these interconnected devices, shedding light on the techniques and tools necessary for both security assessments and defense strategies.

IoT devices, with their diverse functionalities, communicate through various protocols, such as Wi-Fi, Bluetooth, Zigbee, and cellular networks. Gaining control over these devices often requires a deep understanding of their communication methods and potential vulnerabilities. Fortunately, there are several approaches to achieve this control.

One of the fundamental methods for gaining control over IoT devices is exploiting known vulnerabilities. Manufacturers occasionally release devices with inherent security flaws or vulnerabilities in their firmware. Ethical hackers and security professionals can leverage these weaknesses using Metasploit or other penetration testing tools to access and manipulate the devices.

Another avenue for asserting control over IoT devices is by reverse engineering their firmware. IoT devices typically run specialized software, and analyzing this firmware can reveal insights into their functionality and potential security weaknesses. Reverse engineering tools and techniques help security experts understand how these devices operate and discover vulnerabilities that can be exploited.

Additionally, IoT devices often rely on web interfaces or mobile applications for user interaction. These interfaces can serve as entry points for attackers. By conducting security assessments of the web interfaces or mobile apps associated with IoT devices, security professionals can identify vulnerabilities that may allow unauthorized access or control.

Social engineering is another method that malicious actors can use to gain control over IoT devices. This involves manipulating individuals into revealing sensitive information or performing actions that compromise device security. Security awareness and education are essential in countering social engineering attacks.

In some cases, IoT devices may have weak or default credentials that can be easily exploited. By conducting password attacks, such as brute force or dictionary attacks, attackers can gain unauthorized access to these devices. Security experts must assess and strengthen password policies to prevent such incidents.

Once control is established over an IoT device, maintaining access is crucial for further exploration and security assessment. Post-exploitation modules in Metasploit can be used to establish persistence on the compromised device, ensuring that access remains even after reboots or updates.

It's important to note that gaining control over IoT devices should only be done ethically and with proper authorization. Unauthorized access or control of IoT devices is illegal and unethical, potentially resulting in legal consequences. Ethical hackers and security professionals must obtain explicit permission from device owners or manufacturers before conducting assessments.

IoT device manufacturers play a significant role in enhancing security. They should prioritize secure design practices, regularly update firmware to patch vulnerabilities, and encourage responsible disclosure of security flaws. Manufacturers can also benefit from conducting penetration testing and security assessments to identify and rectify potential weaknesses in their devices.

Furthermore, end-users have a role to play in securing IoT devices. They should change default credentials, keep firmware updated, and be cautious about sharing sensitive information with IoT devices. Being aware of potential security risks and practicing good cybersecurity hygiene can go a long way in safeguarding these devices.

In summary, gaining control over IoT devices is a multifaceted process that requires a combination of technical skills, tools, and ethical considerations. Whether for security assessments or defense strategies, it's crucial to approach IoT device control with a responsible and authorized mindset. By doing so, we can work towards securing the ever-expanding landscape of interconnected devices and ensuring that the benefits of IoT technology are enjoyed without compromising security and privacy.

Chapter 8: Securing Wireless and IoT Environments

Securing wireless networks is of paramount importance in today's interconnected world. With the proliferation of wireless technologies, ensuring the confidentiality, integrity, and availability of network resources has become a complex and ever-evolving challenge. Next, we will explore strategies and best practices for securing wireless networks, providing you with the knowledge and tools to protect your organization's critical assets.

One of the foundational elements of wireless network security is the use of strong encryption. Encryption transforms data into an unreadable format, making it indecipherable to unauthorized parties. Implementing robust encryption protocols, such as WPA3 for Wi-Fi networks, is essential to safeguarding wireless communication.

Furthermore, it's essential to change default passwords and credentials on wireless devices. Manufacturers often provide default usernames and passwords, which, if left unchanged, can be exploited by attackers. By replacing default credentials with strong, unique passwords, you reduce the risk of unauthorized access.

Segmentation is another vital strategy for securing wireless networks. Segmentation involves dividing a network into smaller, isolated segments or VLANs (Virtual Local Area Networks). This practice limits the lateral movement of attackers within the network, preventing them from easily accessing sensitive areas.

Implementing network access controls is crucial for wireless network security. Utilizing technologies like

Network Access Control (NAC), you can enforce policies that govern which devices are allowed to connect to the network and under what conditions. This ensures that only authorized devices gain access.

Regularly updating firmware and software is an often-overlooked aspect of wireless network security. Manufacturers release updates to address known vulnerabilities and enhance security. Staying up-to-date with these patches is essential to mitigate potential risks.

Wireless Intrusion Detection Systems (IDS) and Intrusion Prevention Systems (IPS) are valuable tools for monitoring and protecting wireless networks. These systems can detect and respond to suspicious activities, such as unauthorized access attempts or rogue devices.

Implementing strong authentication methods, such as multi-factor authentication (MFA), adds an extra layer of security to wireless networks. MFA requires users to provide multiple forms of verification before granting access, making it significantly more challenging for attackers to compromise accounts.

Physical security measures are also important in wireless network security. Access points and network infrastructure should be physically protected to prevent tampering or unauthorized access.

Regularly auditing and monitoring network traffic is essential for identifying anomalous behavior. By analyzing network traffic patterns and logs, you can detect and respond to potential security incidents promptly.

User education and awareness play a significant role in wireless network security. Training employees and users on best practices, such as not sharing credentials and recognizing phishing attempts, can help prevent security breaches.

Implementing a strong incident response plan is critical for addressing security incidents when they occur. This plan should outline the steps to take in case of a security breach and designate responsible individuals or teams for incident resolution.

Wireless networks should be regularly assessed through penetration testing and vulnerability scanning. These assessments help identify weaknesses that may be exploited by attackers. Addressing these vulnerabilities enhances network security.

Security policies and procedures should be well-documented and communicated to all stakeholders. These policies should cover topics such as acceptable use, data handling, and incident reporting.

When it comes to wireless network security, it's essential to strike a balance between security and usability. Overly restrictive security measures can hinder productivity, while lax security can expose the network to risks. Finding the right balance tailored to your organization's needs is key.

Lastly, consider implementing a robust monitoring and alerting system. This system can provide real-time notifications of suspicious activities, allowing for immediate response and mitigation.

In summary, securing wireless networks is an ongoing effort that requires a multifaceted approach. By implementing strong encryption, changing default credentials, segmenting the network, and using network access controls, you can establish a solid foundation for security. Regular updates, intrusion detection, strong authentication, and user education further enhance network protection. Combining these strategies with physical security, incident response planning, regular assessments, and well-documented policies creates a comprehensive security posture that helps safeguard your wireless networks in an increasingly interconnected world. Securing Internet of Things (IoT) devices has become increasingly critical as these devices have become integral to our daily lives. IoT devices encompass a wide range of products, from smart thermostats and cameras to industrial sensors and medical devices. Ensuring the security of these devices is essential to protect both individual privacy and the integrity of connected networks.

First and foremost, it's vital to keep IoT device firmware up to date. Manufacturers release updates to address vulnerabilities and improve security. Regularly applying these updates helps mitigate potential risks and ensures that your devices are running the latest security patches.

Changing default passwords and credentials is a fundamental practice in IoT device security. Manufacturers often provide default usernames and passwords that can be easily exploited by attackers if left unchanged. Replacing these defaults with strong, unique passwords is a simple yet effective security measure.

Network segmentation is a crucial strategy for securing IoT devices. Isolating IoT devices from the primary network can prevent potential attackers from gaining access to sensitive data or other connected devices. This segregation limits the attack surface and minimizes the potential impact of a breach.

Implementing strong authentication mechanisms is essential for IoT device security. Multi-factor authentication (MFA) adds an extra layer of protection by requiring users to provide multiple forms of verification before gaining access to the device or its associated services.

Regularly monitoring network traffic and device behavior is vital for early detection of anomalies or potential security incidents. Establishing baseline behavior for IoT devices and setting up alerts for deviations can help identify suspicious activity.

Encryption plays a critical role in protecting data transmitted between IoT devices and the cloud or other endpoints. Utilizing strong encryption protocols ensures that data remains confidential and cannot be easily intercepted by malicious actors.

Device access controls should be enforced to restrict access to authorized users or devices only. These controls can help prevent unauthorized users or devices from interacting with IoT devices or changing their settings. Implementing a robust incident response plan specific to IoT devices is essential. This plan should outline the steps to take in case of a security incident, including isolation of affected devices, notification of relevant parties, and investigation procedures.

Physical security measures should not be overlooked. Physical access to IoT devices can lead to tampering or theft of sensitive information. Properly securing IoT devices in a physical location can mitigate these risks.

Regularly conducting vulnerability assessments and penetration testing on IoT devices can help identify and remediate security weaknesses. These assessments should cover both the device itself and any associated software or services. User education and awareness are crucial aspects of IoT device security. Users should be informed about the risks associated with IoT devices, such as privacy concerns and potential vulnerabilities. They should also be educated on best practices for device usage and security.

Collaboration with device manufacturers is essential. Manufacturers should be encouraged to prioritize security in the design and production of IoT devices. Transparency in terms of security practices and policies is also beneficial for consumers.

Regulatory compliance should not be overlooked. Depending on your region and industry, there may be specific regulations or standards that govern IoT device security. Ensuring compliance with these requirements is vital.

Lastly, it's essential to consider the end-of-life (EOL) and disposal of IoT devices. Properly decommissioning and disposing of devices ensures that they do not pose a security risk once they are no longer in use.

In summary, securing IoT devices requires a comprehensive approach that encompasses firmware updates, password management, network segmentation, strong authentication, monitoring, encryption, access controls, incident response planning, physical security, vulnerability assessments, user education, collaboration with manufacturers, regulatory compliance, and proper EOL practices. By implementing these best practices, individuals and organizations can enhance the security of IoT devices and protect against potential threats in an increasingly connected world.

Chapter 9: Advanced Attacks on Wireless and IoT

Exploring the realm of advanced wireless attacks opens up a world of possibilities and challenges in the field of cybersecurity. These attacks are the next level of wireless security testing, where experienced professionals delve deep into the vulnerabilities of wireless networks to identify weaknesses, assess risks, and enhance defenses.

One of the more advanced wireless attack techniques is known as rogue access point creation. This involves an attacker setting up a malicious access point that mimics a legitimate network. Unsuspecting users may connect to this rogue access point, exposing their data and credentials to the attacker.

Deauthentication attacks are another advanced technique where an attacker sends deauthentication frames to legitimate devices on a network, forcing them to disconnect from their access point. This can lead to disruptions in network services and create opportunities for further attacks.

Evil Twin attacks take rogue access points a step further by not only mimicking a legitimate network but also capturing data transmitted between the victim and the attacker-controlled access point. This type of attack can be particularly effective in capturing sensitive information.

Wireless jamming is an advanced attack that involves flooding a wireless network with noise, disrupting communications between devices and access points. This can lead to network outages and impair the functionality of connected devices.

Cracking WPA/WPA2 encryption is a challenging but highly effective advanced wireless attack. Attackers use powerful computing resources to crack the encryption keys protecting a Wi-Fi network, allowing them to decrypt network traffic and potentially gain access to sensitive information.

Another advanced wireless attack involves bypassing captive portal login pages. Captive portals are commonly used in public Wi-Fi networks, requiring users to sign in or accept terms and conditions before gaining access. Attackers may employ techniques to bypass these portals and gain unauthorized access.

MAC address spoofing is an advanced technique used to impersonate a legitimate device on a network by changing the device's MAC address. This can allow an attacker to gain unauthorized access and evade network security measures.

Advanced wireless attacks also include leveraging vulnerabilities in Wi-Fi protocols and standards. For example, attackers may target vulnerabilities in the Wi-Fi Protected Setup (WPS) protocol to gain access to a network. Similarly, the KRACK attack demonstrated weaknesses in the WPA2 protocol, allowing attackers to intercept and decrypt network traffic.

Spectrum analysis attacks involve the manipulation of radio frequencies and signal interference to disrupt wireless networks. Attackers can use specialized equipment to perform these attacks, causing network outages or degrading performance.

Furthermore, advanced attackers may exploit zero-day vulnerabilities in wireless devices or access points. Zero-day vulnerabilities are those for which no patch or fix is available, making them particularly attractive targets for attackers seeking to gain an advantage.

Advanced wireless attacks are not limited to Wi-Fi networks; they also extend to other wireless technologies such as Bluetooth and Zigbee. Attackers can target vulnerabilities in these protocols to compromise devices and networks.

As organizations continue to adopt IoT devices, advanced wireless attacks on these devices are becoming more prevalent. Attackers can target vulnerabilities in IoT protocols, firmware, and device configurations to gain unauthorized access or disrupt IoT networks.

Defending against advanced wireless attacks requires a multifaceted approach. Organizations should regularly update firmware and apply security patches to wireless devices and access points. Strong encryption and authentication mechanisms should be implemented to protect network traffic.

Network monitoring and intrusion detection systems can help detect and respond to advanced wireless attacks in real-time. Additionally, organizations should educate their users about the risks of connecting to unknown or unsecured wireless networks and provide guidelines for secure wireless usage.

Implementing network segmentation can limit the impact of wireless attacks by isolating critical assets from less secure areas of the network. This can prevent attackers from moving laterally within the network once they gain access.

Regular security assessments and penetration testing can help identify vulnerabilities and weaknesses in wireless networks, allowing organizations to proactively address these issues before they can be exploited by attackers.

In summary, advanced wireless attacks represent a significant challenge in the ever-evolving landscape of cybersecurity. These attacks exploit vulnerabilities in wireless networks, protocols, and devices to gain unauthorized access, intercept data, disrupt services, and compromise security. Defending against advanced wireless attacks requires a proactive and comprehensive security strategy that includes regular updates, strong encryption, network monitoring, user education, network segmentation, and security assessments. By staying informed about the latest threats and taking proactive measures, organizations can enhance their wireless security posture and protect against advanced wireless attacks.

As we delve into the realm of IoT security, it becomes increasingly clear that targeted exploitation of IoT devices is a topic of paramount importance in the ever-evolving landscape of cybersecurity. IoT, or the Internet of Things, has ushered in a new era of connectivity, enabling devices of all types to communicate and share data over the internet. While this interconnectedness offers tremendous benefits in terms of convenience and efficiency, it also presents significant security challenges.

To understand the concept of targeted exploitation of IoT devices, we must first recognize the unique characteristics and vulnerabilities inherent to these devices. IoT devices encompass a vast array of objects, from smart thermostats and wearable fitness trackers to industrial sensors and autonomous vehicles. They often have limited computing resources, operate on diverse communication protocols, and may lack robust security features.

One key aspect of targeted exploitation in the context of IoT is the selection of specific devices or systems as the focus of an attack. Unlike broad-scale, indiscriminate attacks, which cast a wide net in hopes of compromising any available device, targeted exploitation involves identifying particular devices or device types that hold value for an attacker. These devices may be chosen for various reasons, including their potential to provide access to a broader network, sensitive data, or control over physical systems.

Targeted IoT exploitation can encompass a range of attack vectors. One common approach involves identifying known vulnerabilities in the firmware or software running on IoT devices. Vulnerabilities may exist due to insecure coding practices, outdated software, or inadequate security mechanisms. Attackers actively search for these vulnerabilities and exploit them to gain unauthorized access or control.

Another facet of targeted exploitation involves the manipulation of IoT device communication protocols. Many IoT devices rely on wireless communication standards like Zigbee, Bluetooth, or Wi-Fi to connect to networks and other devices. Attackers may intercept, manipulate, or inject malicious traffic into these communications, disrupting device functionality or compromising data integrity.

In some cases, attackers may seek to compromise IoT devices to create botnets. Botnets are networks of compromised devices that can be controlled by an attacker, often for malicious purposes like launching

Distributed Denial of Service (DDoS) attacks or sending spam. IoT devices with weak security measures can be attractive targets for building botnets due to their large numbers and potential vulnerability.

The consequences of successful targeted IoT exploitation can be far-reaching. In industrial settings, for instance, attackers could compromise IoT sensors or controllers to disrupt critical processes or damage equipment. In a smart home environment, unauthorized access to connected devices like security cameras or door locks could compromise personal privacy and security. Furthermore, compromised IoT devices can serve as a launching pad for attacks on larger networks or systems.

Mitigating the risks associated with targeted IoT exploitation requires a multifaceted approach. First and foremost, manufacturers must prioritize security in the design and development of IoT devices. This includes implementing secure coding practices, regularly updating device firmware to address vulnerabilities, and providing mechanisms for users to change default passwords and update software.

Network segmentation can also be an effective strategy to limit the potential impact of an IoT compromise. By isolating IoT devices from critical network segments, organizations can contain the effects of a breach and prevent lateral movement by attackers.

Furthermore, organizations should deploy intrusion detection systems and regularly monitor IoT device traffic for signs of malicious activity. Anomalies in device behavior or communication patterns can be indicative of a security breach.

User education plays a crucial role in mitigating the risks of targeted IoT exploitation. Users should be aware of the security implications of their IoT devices and take steps to secure them, such as changing default passwords and keeping firmware up to date. Additionally, organizations should establish clear security policies and procedures for the use of IoT devices in both personal and professional settings.

In summary, targeted exploitation of IoT devices is a critical concern in the field of cybersecurity. As IoT continues to proliferate and play an increasingly integral role in our daily lives, the security of these devices becomes paramount. By understanding the unique challenges posed by IoT devices, implementing robust security measures, and fostering a culture of security awareness, we can mitigate the risks associated with targeted IoT exploitation and ensure a safer and more secure IoT ecosystem for all.

Chapter 10: Reporting and Best Practices

Effective reporting of wireless and IoT security findings is a crucial aspect of any cybersecurity assessment. It serves as the bridge between the technical details of a security assessment and the understanding of key stakeholders, including executives, IT teams, and regulatory bodies. Next, we will explore the importance of clear and concise reporting, discuss the key components of a comprehensive security report, and offer guidelines for effectively communicating security findings.

Security assessments, whether focused on wireless networks or IoT devices, generate a wealth of technical data and findings. While this data is valuable for technical teams responsible for remediation, it can be overwhelming and incomprehensible to those who lack specialized knowledge in cybersecurity. Effective reporting bridges this gap by translating technical details into actionable insights and recommendations.

One of the primary goals of reporting is to provide a clear and accurate representation of the security posture of wireless networks or IoT environments. This includes identifying vulnerabilities, assessing their severity, and prioritizing them based on potential impact and likelihood of exploitation. The report should also highlight any successful exploits or unauthorized access to wireless or IoT systems.

A well-structured security report typically begins with an executive summary. This concise section is intended for non-technical stakeholders and provides a high-level overview of the assessment, including key findings, risks, and recommended actions. It serves as an entry point to the report, offering decision-makers a quick understanding of the security assessment's implications.

Following the executive summary, the report delves into the technical details of the assessment. This section includes a comprehensive description of the assessment methodology, including the tools and techniques used, as well as a detailed account of vulnerabilities and their associated risks. Vulnerabilities should be categorized by severity, allowing organizations to prioritize remediation efforts effectively.

To facilitate a clear understanding of the findings, security reports often include supporting evidence. This may include screenshots, logs, and other artifacts that demonstrate the presence and impact of vulnerabilities or successful exploits. Providing evidence helps validate the findings and aids in their resolution.

In addition to documenting vulnerabilities, the report should offer practical recommendations for remediation. These recommendations should be actionable and tailored to the organization's specific context. For example, if a wireless network assessment uncovers weak encryption protocols, the report should recommend upgrading to stronger encryption methods and provide guidance on how to implement this change.

When reporting on IoT security, it's essential to consider the unique challenges and characteristics of IoT devices. These devices often have limited processing power and storage, which can impact the feasibility of certain security measures. Reports should address these limitations and suggest strategies to secure IoT devices effectively.

Furthermore, a comprehensive security report should outline a roadmap for improving the security posture of wireless networks or IoT environments. This roadmap should prioritize actions based on risk and provide a timeline for implementation. It may also include recommendations for ongoing monitoring and periodic security assessments.

Beyond the technical details, effective reporting should consider the audience. Different stakeholders have varying levels of technical expertise and interests. Reports should be tailored to the needs of each group, providing technical details for IT and security teams while offering high-level insights for executives and non-technical staff.

Clarity and readability are paramount in reporting. Complex technical jargon should be avoided or explained in plain language. Visual aids such as charts and graphs can help convey information more effectively. The report should also adhere to a consistent structure, making it easy for readers to navigate and locate specific information.

In some cases, security reports may need to meet regulatory or compliance requirements. Organizations in industries like healthcare, finance, or government may have specific reporting standards to follow. It's essential to ensure that the report aligns with these requirements to maintain compliance.

Effective reporting is not a one-time event but an ongoing process. Organizations should regularly assess their wireless networks and IoT environments and provide updated reports as new vulnerabilities are discovered, and security measures are implemented. Continuous monitoring and reporting help ensure that security remains robust over time.

In summary, effective reporting of wireless and IoT security findings is a critical component of any cybersecurity assessment. It serves to bridge the gap between technical details and actionable insights, facilitating informed decision-making and risk mitigation. By tailoring reports to the needs of various stakeholders, providing clear evidence, and offering practical recommendations, organizations can enhance their security posture and protect their wireless networks and IoT devices effectively.

Security best practices are essential for safeguarding wireless and IoT environments in today's interconnected world. These practices are a set of guidelines and strategies that organizations can follow to mitigate risks and protect their networks and devices from cyber threats. Next, we will explore key security best practices for both wireless networks and IoT environments, helping you establish a strong foundation for security.

First and foremost, it's crucial to establish a robust security policy for your wireless network and IoT devices. This policy should outline your organization's approach to security, define roles and responsibilities, and set clear expectations for users. Having a well-documented security policy provides a framework for implementing security measures and ensures that everyone in the organization understands their role in maintaining security.

Access control is a fundamental aspect of security. For wireless networks, it's essential to implement strong authentication methods, such as WPA3 for Wi-Fi, to ensure that only authorized users can connect. Multi-factor authentication (MFA) adds an extra layer of security by requiring users to provide multiple forms of verification, like a password and a fingerprint, before gaining access.

For IoT devices, access control can be more challenging due to the diversity of devices and their limited capabilities. However, implementing secure access controls for IoT devices is essential. This may involve using unique, strong passwords, restricting device access to specific IP addresses or networks, and regularly updating device credentials.

Network segmentation is a powerful security practice that involves dividing a network into isolated segments or VLANs. By segmenting your network, you can contain potential threats and limit lateral movement by attackers. In IoT environments, this is especially important as it can prevent a compromised device from accessing critical systems.

Regular software updates and patch management are critical for both wireless networks and IoT devices. Unpatched software is a common entry point for cyberattacks, so it's essential to keep all devices and systems up-to-date with the latest security patches. Many IoT devices lack automatic update mechanisms, so organizations must actively monitor and update these devices.

Network monitoring and intrusion detection systems are valuable tools for identifying and responding to security threats. These systems can alert you to suspicious activities and provide insights into potential vulnerabilities. In IoT environments, monitoring is essential for detecting anomalies in device behavior, which may indicate a compromise.

Encryption plays a significant role in securing wireless and IoT communications. Encrypting data in transit and at rest ensures that even if an attacker intercepts information, they cannot decipher it without the encryption key. Using protocols like HTTPS for web traffic and strong encryption algorithms for IoT communications is vital.

Implementing firewalls and intrusion prevention systems (IPS) can help protect wireless networks and IoT environments from unauthorized access and attacks. Firewalls can filter incoming and outgoing traffic, while IPS can detect and block malicious activities in real-time. These security measures add layers of defense to your network.

Regular security training and awareness programs for employees are essential to prevent security breaches. Many cyberattacks target human vulnerabilities, such as phishing emails or social engineering. Educating employees about the latest threats and best practices can significantly reduce the risk of falling victim to these attacks.

For IoT environments, it's crucial to assess the security of IoT devices before integrating them into your network. Not all IoT devices are created equal, and some may have known vulnerabilities. Conducting a thorough security evaluation and risk assessment of IoT devices helps identify potential risks and allows for informed decision-making.

Security audits and penetration testing are proactive measures to identify vulnerabilities and weaknesses in your wireless and IoT environments. Regularly testing your security controls and configurations can help you address issues before they are exploited by malicious actors.

For wireless networks, it's wise to disable unnecessary services and features that can be exploited by attackers. Features like remote management interfaces should be turned off if not needed, reducing the attack surface.

In IoT environments, strong device lifecycle management is essential. This includes securely provisioning devices, monitoring their behavior throughout their lifecycle, and decommissioning them properly when they are no longer in use. Unmanaged IoT devices can become security liabilities.

Secure authentication and authorization mechanisms should be implemented for both wireless and IoT environments. Access should be granted on a need-to-know basis, and privileges should be limited to prevent unauthorized access or actions.

In wireless networks, regular security assessments and vulnerability scanning can help identify weak points in your security posture. These assessments should be conducted by skilled professionals who can uncover potential vulnerabilities and provide recommendations for mitigation.

In IoT environments, data privacy should be a priority. Ensure that sensitive data collected by IoT devices is stored and transmitted securely. Comply with data protection regulations and consider encryption and anonymization techniques to protect user privacy.

Finally, incident response plans are essential for both wireless networks and IoT environments. Despite all preventive measures, security incidents can still occur. A well-prepared incident response plan can help you detect, contain, and mitigate the impact of security breaches.

In summary, security best practices are crucial for protecting wireless networks and IoT environments from a wide range of cyber threats. By establishing a robust security policy, implementing access controls, segmenting networks, keeping software up-to-date, monitoring for threats, and following other best practices, organizations can significantly enhance their security posture. It's essential to continually evaluate and adapt security measures to address evolving threats and vulnerabilities in an ever-changing digital landscape.

Understanding emerging threat trends and patterns is essential in today's rapidly evolving cybersecurity landscape. As technology advances and cybercriminals become more sophisticated, staying ahead of new threats is critical to maintaining a strong security posture. Next, we will explore some of the most significant emerging threat trends and patterns, helping you prepare for and defend against them.

One notable trend is the increasing prevalence of ransomware attacks. Ransomware is a type of malware that encrypts a victim's data and demands a ransom for the decryption key. What makes this threat particularly concerning is the growing sophistication of ransomware gangs and their ability to target organizations of all sizes. Understanding how ransomware operates and having robust backup and recovery strategies in place is crucial for mitigating this threat.

Another emerging trend is the rise of supply chain attacks. Cybercriminals are increasingly targeting the software and hardware supply chain to compromise products before they even reach end-users. These attacks can have far-reaching consequences, as they can affect numerous organizations that rely on the compromised supply chain. Vigilance and thorough vetting of suppliers and their security practices are essential.

Phishing attacks remain a prevalent threat, but they have evolved. While traditional phishing emails are still common, attackers are now using more sophisticated techniques, such as spear-phishing and business email compromise (BEC). These attacks often involve extensive reconnaissance to craft convincing messages that deceive even vigilant users. Employee training and awareness are essential defenses against these evolving phishing tactics.

The Internet of Things (IoT) introduces new attack vectors, making it an emerging threat trend. IoT devices are becoming ubiquitous in both homes and businesses, but many lack robust security features. Cybercriminals are exploiting these weaknesses to compromise networks and launch attacks. Organizations should implement strict security controls for IoT devices and regularly update their firmware.

Cyberattacks targeting critical infrastructure are another growing concern. Attackers are increasingly focusing on essential services such as power grids, water supply systems, and transportation networks. Disrupting these critical systems can have severe consequences. Protecting critical infrastructure requires close collaboration between government agencies, private sector organizations, and cybersecurity experts.

Cloud security is also a significant emerging concern. As more organizations migrate to cloud environments, cybercriminals are following them. Misconfigured cloud resources, inadequate access controls, and weak authentication can lead to data breaches and other security incidents. Organizations should adopt a robust cloud security posture and regularly audit their cloud configurations.

Zero-day vulnerabilities are a persistent threat trend. These vulnerabilities are unknown to software vendors and have no available patches. Cybercriminals actively seek and exploit zero-days to gain unauthorized access to systems. Staying informed about the latest threats and promptly applying patches when they become available is essential for defense.

Artificial intelligence (AI) and machine learning (ML) are not only tools for defenders but also for attackers. Cybercriminals are using AI and ML to automate attacks, evade detection, and craft convincing phishing emails. Security professionals must leverage AI and ML to enhance their threat detection capabilities and stay ahead of cybercriminals.

The expansion of remote work has opened up new attack surfaces. With employees working from various locations and using personal devices, organizations face increased risks. Securing remote work environments, implementing strong authentication, and providing secure remote access solutions are critical for defending against these threats.

Nation-state actors continue to be a significant threat. State-sponsored cyberattacks can have geopolitical implications and cause substantial harm to targeted organizations. Organizations should be prepared for advanced persistent threats (APTs) and have incident response plans in place to mitigate the impact of such attacks.

Cryptojacking is a relatively new threat trend where attackers use the computing power of compromised devices to mine cryptocurrencies without the owner's consent. While not as damaging as some other threats, cryptojacking can impact system performance and increase operational costs. Detecting and preventing cryptojacking requires robust endpoint security.

Another emerging threat is the use of deepfakes and synthetic media for social engineering attacks. Deepfakes can create convincing fake audio and video recordings of individuals, making it challenging to distinguish real communications from fraudulent ones. Organizations should be vigilant and establish verification procedures for sensitive communications.

The convergence of cyber and physical threats is an emerging concern. Cyberattacks can have real-world consequences, as seen in incidents targeting industrial control systems and critical infrastructure. Preparing for and responding to cyber-physical threats requires a multidisciplinary approach involving cybersecurity and physical security experts.

Finally, the regulatory landscape for cybersecurity is evolving rapidly. Governments worldwide are enacting stricter data protection laws and imposing hefty fines for non-compliance. Organizations must stay informed about relevant regulations, such as the General Data Protection Regulation (GDPR) and the California Consumer Privacy Act (CCPA), and ensure they meet compliance requirements.

In summary, understanding and addressing emerging threat trends and patterns is essential for organizations striving to protect their digital assets and data. By staying informed about these evolving threats and implementing proactive security measures, organizations can reduce their risk exposure and better defend against cyberattacks. The cybersecurity landscape will continue to evolve, making ongoing vigilance and adaptation critical components of effective defense strategies.

BOOK 4
METASPLOIT MASTERCLASS
ADVANCED THREAT DETECTION AND DEFENSE

ROB BOTWRIGHT

Chapter 1: Understanding the Threat Landscape

The current threat landscape in cybersecurity is marked by a level of complexity and sophistication that was unimaginable just a few years ago. Cyber threats have evolved significantly, and their impact on individuals, businesses, and even nations is profound. Understanding the implications of this evolving landscape is crucial for effectively addressing the challenges it presents.

One of the most significant impacts of the current threat landscape is the financial cost associated with cyberattacks. Businesses of all sizes are facing substantial financial losses due to data breaches, ransomware attacks, and other cyber incidents. These losses include not only the direct costs of incident response, but also the expenses related to regulatory fines, legal fees, and reputational damage.

The reputational damage caused by cyberattacks can be severe and long-lasting. When customer data is compromised, trust erodes, and it can take years to rebuild a damaged reputation. This impact goes beyond financial losses and affects a company's ability to attract and retain customers.

National security is another critical concern in the current threat landscape. Nation-state actors are actively engaged in cyber espionage, sabotage, and disruption campaigns. These attacks can target government agencies, critical infrastructure, and private sector organizations. The implications for national security are far-reaching, as cyberattacks can have geopolitical consequences.

The proliferation of cybercrime-as-a-service has democratized cyberattacks. Even individuals with limited technical skills can purchase malware and launch attacks. This commoditization of cybercrime makes it easier for cybercriminals to target a wide range of victims, from individuals to small businesses and large enterprises.

The threat landscape is also characterized by increasingly sophisticated and targeted attacks. Cybercriminals conduct extensive reconnaissance to gather information about their targets, enabling them to craft convincing spear-phishing emails and tailored attack strategies. These targeted attacks are often difficult to detect and defend against.

Ransomware attacks have become a significant driver of cyber insurance costs. The frequency and severity of ransomware incidents have surged, and the ransom demands have grown exponentially. Organizations that do not have robust backup and recovery strategies in place can find themselves in dire situations when faced with a ransomware attack.

Regulatory compliance is a growing concern in the current threat landscape. Governments worldwide are enacting stricter data protection laws, and organizations must ensure compliance with these regulations. The European Union's General Data Protection Regulation (GDPR) and the California Consumer Privacy Act (CCPA) are just two examples of comprehensive data protection laws with significant penalties for non-compliance.

Supply chain attacks pose a pervasive threat to organizations. Cybercriminals are increasingly targeting the software and hardware supply chain to compromise products before they reach end-users. This tactic can impact numerous organizations that rely on the compromised supply chain, making supply chain security a critical concern.

The Internet of Things (IoT) introduces new vulnerabilities and attack vectors. IoT devices are ubiquitous in homes and businesses, but many lack robust security features. Cybercriminals exploit these weaknesses to compromise networks and launch attacks. Protecting against IoT-related threats requires organizations to implement strict security controls for these devices.

Zero-day vulnerabilities, which are unknown to software vendors and have no available patches, are a persistent concern. Cybercriminals actively seek and exploit zero-days to gain unauthorized access to systems. Organizations must stay informed about the latest threats and promptly apply patches when they become available.

The current threat landscape also includes the use of artificial intelligence (AI) and machine learning (ML) by both attackers and defenders. Cybercriminals use AI and ML to automate attacks, evade detection, and optimize their strategies. On the defensive side, security professionals leverage AI and ML to enhance threat detection and response capabilities.

Remote work has introduced new attack surfaces. With the rise of remote work, employees are accessing corporate networks and data from various locations and using personal devices. Organizations must secure remote work environments, implement strong authentication, and provide secure remote access solutions to mitigate the associated risks.

The convergence of cyber and physical threats is a growing concern in the current threat landscape. Cyberattacks can have real-world consequences, particularly when targeting critical infrastructure. Preparing for and responding to cyber-physical threats requires a multidisciplinary approach that involves both cybersecurity and physical security experts.

In summary, the impact of the current threat landscape on individuals, organizations, and nations cannot be underestimated. The financial, reputational, and national security implications of cyberattacks are profound. To navigate this landscape successfully, organizations must adopt a proactive and comprehensive approach to cybersecurity that encompasses technology, policies, employee training, and incident response planning. Staying informed about emerging threats and continuously improving security measures is essential in this ever-evolving environment.

In the constantly evolving landscape of cybersecurity, emerging threat trends and patterns play a pivotal role in shaping the way organizations defend against cyberattacks. These trends shed light on the evolving tactics, techniques, and procedures (TTPs) employed by cybercriminals and threat actors. To effectively navigate this complex terrain, it is essential to delve into these emerging threat trends and patterns and understand their implications.

One of the prominent emerging threat trends is the increasing sophistication of ransomware attacks. Ransomware has evolved from being a relatively unsophisticated tool to a highly developed and specialized form of malware. Threat actors are now employing advanced encryption techniques, multi-stage payloads, and evasion tactics that make detection and remediation challenging. This trend is further exacerbated by the growing prevalence of double extortion, where attackers not only encrypt data but also exfiltrate sensitive information, threatening to release it unless a ransom is paid.

Supply chain attacks have gained significant traction in recent years. These attacks involve targeting the software and hardware supply chain to compromise products before they reach end-users. Threat actors exploit vulnerabilities in the supply chain to inject malware or backdoors into products, which can then be used to compromise the systems of unsuspecting organizations. The SolarWinds supply chain attack is a notable example that underscored the far-reaching impact of such incidents.

Cyber-physical threats are becoming more pronounced as critical infrastructure and industrial control systems (ICS) are increasingly connected to the internet. Threat actors are actively looking for ways to breach these systems, which control essential services like energy, water, and transportation. Successful attacks on critical infrastructure can have dire real-world consequences, highlighting the urgency of securing these systems against cyber threats.

Zero-day vulnerabilities, which are unknown to software vendors and have no available patches, continue to be a significant concern. Cybercriminals actively seek and exploit these vulnerabilities to gain unauthorized access to systems. Security researchers and vendors often engage in a race against time to discover and patch these vulnerabilities before they can be exploited maliciously.

The use of artificial intelligence (AI) and machine learning (ML) in cyberattacks is on the rise. Threat actors are leveraging AI and ML to automate various aspects of their attacks, from crafting convincing spear-phishing emails to evading detection by security tools. This trend makes it increasingly challenging for traditional rule-based security solutions to keep pace with evolving attack techniques.

Phishing attacks remain a prevalent and effective method for threat actors to compromise organizations. These attacks often target individuals with social engineering tactics, attempting to trick them into revealing sensitive information or clicking on malicious links. Phishing campaigns have become more sophisticated, employing carefully crafted emails and persuasive lures.

State-sponsored cyber espionage continues to be a significant threat to governments and organizations worldwide. Nation-state actors conduct highly targeted campaigns to steal sensitive information, gain a strategic advantage, or disrupt their adversaries. Attribution of these attacks can be challenging, as threat actors go to great lengths to conceal their identities.

The increasing reliance on cloud services and infrastructure has given rise to cloud-specific threats. Misconfigured cloud resources, inadequate access controls, and weak authentication mechanisms have exposed organizations to data breaches and unauthorized access. Ensuring the secure configuration and management of cloud environments is paramount to mitigating these risks.

Deepfake technology, which uses AI to create realistic but fabricated audio and video content, poses new challenges for cybersecurity. Threat actors can use deepfakes to impersonate individuals, potentially leading to identity theft and social engineering attacks. Detecting and mitigating the impact of deepfakes requires innovative solutions and increased awareness.

The convergence of cyber threats with geopolitical tensions and conflicts has blurred the lines between state-sponsored and financially motivated attacks. Attribution becomes more complex when threat actors operate with political motivations, further complicating the threat landscape.

In summary, staying ahead of emerging threat trends and patterns is essential for organizations and security professionals. Cybersecurity strategies must continuously evolve to address the evolving tactics of threat actors. This includes investing in advanced threat detection and response capabilities, improving employee awareness and training, and collaborating with the broader cybersecurity community to share threat intelligence and best practices. By understanding the shifting landscape of cyber threats, organizations can better protect themselves and their stakeholders from the ever-present dangers of the digital world.

Chapter 2: Fundamentals of Threat Detection

Understanding the principles of threat detection is essential in the ongoing battle against cyber threats and attacks, as organizations increasingly rely on digital technology for their operations and services. Threat detection is the proactive process of identifying signs and indicators of potential security incidents, breaches, or malicious activities within an organization's network and systems. These principles serve as the foundation for establishing effective threat detection capabilities and strengthening an organization's overall cybersecurity posture.

One fundamental principle of threat detection is visibility. To effectively detect threats, organizations must have comprehensive visibility into their network, systems, and data. This means continuously monitoring all network traffic, including internal and external communications, to identify anomalous patterns or behaviors that may indicate a security issue. Without adequate visibility, threats can go undetected, leading to potential breaches and data loss.

Another critical principle is the use of threat intelligence. Threat intelligence refers to the information and insights collected and analyzed about current and emerging cyber threats. By leveraging threat intelligence from various sources, including industry reports, government agencies, and cybersecurity vendors, organizations can gain a better understanding of the tactics, techniques, and procedures (TTPs) employed by threat actors. This knowledge is invaluable in improving threat detection capabilities by aligning them with the latest threat landscape.

Continuous monitoring is a core principle that emphasizes the importance of real-time or near-real-time monitoring of network activities. Threats evolve rapidly, and timely detection is crucial for effective response. Implementing automated monitoring solutions and security information and event management (SIEM) systems can help organizations identify suspicious activities as they occur, enabling faster response and mitigation efforts.

The principle of context is integral to accurate threat detection. Contextual information provides insights into the significance of a detected event. For example, an isolated login failure might not raise immediate concern, but if it's associated with multiple failed login attempts from different locations, it may indicate a coordinated brute-force attack. Contextual analysis allows security teams to prioritize alerts and incidents based on their potential impact and relevance.

Correlation and pattern recognition are vital principles in threat detection. Instead of analyzing individual security events in isolation, organizations should focus on identifying patterns and correlations among events and data points. Advanced analytics and machine learning algorithms can assist in recognizing complex attack patterns and deviations from normal behavior, increasing the accuracy of threat detection.

Scalability is a crucial consideration for threat detection systems. As organizations grow and their digital footprint expands, their threat detection capabilities must be able to scale accordingly. Scalable solutions ensure that monitoring and detection processes remain effective, even as the volume of data and network traffic increases.

Human expertise is an indispensable component of effective threat detection. Skilled cybersecurity professionals play a pivotal role in configuring, monitoring, and interpreting the output of threat detection systems. They are responsible for analyzing alerts, investigating incidents, and responding to threats. Their experience and knowledge enable them to make informed decisions about the severity and potential impact of detected threats.

The principle of integration emphasizes the importance of connecting various security tools and systems to create a holistic threat detection ecosystem. Integrating security solutions such as intrusion detection systems (IDS), endpoint detection and response (EDR) platforms, firewalls, and SIEMs allows for a more comprehensive view of an organization's security posture. Integrated systems can share information and automate responses, reducing the manual effort required to manage threats.

Threat detection is an ongoing process that requires continuous improvement and adaptation. Organizations should regularly review and update their threat detection strategies to address emerging threats and vulnerabilities. Conducting post-incident reviews and analyzing the effectiveness of detection and response efforts can lead to refinements in threat detection capabilities.

Lastly, the principle of collaboration underscores the importance of information sharing and cooperation among organizations, industries, and cybersecurity communities. Threat intelligence sharing and collaboration can help organizations stay informed about emerging threats and benefit from collective knowledge and experience.

In summary, the principles of threat detection serve as a guide for organizations seeking to establish robust and effective security measures. These principles encompass visibility, threat intelligence, continuous monitoring, context, correlation, scalability, human expertise, integration, adaptability, and collaboration. By adhering to these principles and continually enhancing their threat detection capabilities, organizations can better protect themselves from evolving cyber threats and maintain a resilient cybersecurity posture in an increasingly interconnected digital world.

Understanding threat detection technologies and tools is essential in the ever-evolving landscape of cybersecurity, where threats continually adapt and grow in sophistication. These technologies and tools are the frontline defenses that organizations employ to identify and mitigate security incidents, ensuring the protection of sensitive data, intellectual property, and critical infrastructure.

One of the foundational technologies in threat detection is the Intrusion Detection System (IDS). An IDS monitors network traffic for suspicious activities or patterns that may indicate unauthorized access or malicious behavior. IDS can be categorized into two main types: network-based (NIDS) and host-based (HIDS). NIDS passively analyzes network packets, while HIDS monitors activities on individual hosts or endpoints.

A closely related technology to IDS is Intrusion Prevention Systems (IPS). IPS not only detects threats but also takes proactive measures to block or mitigate them in real-time.

It can automatically enforce security policies and rules, making it a critical component of network security.

Security Information and Event Management (SIEM) systems play a pivotal role in threat detection and response. SIEM solutions collect, normalize, and analyze logs and data from various sources, including network devices, servers, and applications. By correlating and aggregating this data, SIEMs provide a holistic view of an organization's security posture, helping to identify unusual activities or potential threats.

Endpoint Detection and Response (EDR) tools focus on monitoring and securing individual endpoints, such as computers and mobile devices. EDR solutions collect detailed telemetry data, enabling organizations to detect advanced threats that might evade traditional antivirus software. They also provide the capability to investigate and respond to incidents at the endpoint level.

Machine learning and artificial intelligence (AI) are increasingly integrated into threat detection technologies. These advanced algorithms can analyze vast amounts of data and identify patterns and anomalies that may be indicative of security threats. Machine learning models can adapt and improve over time, enhancing detection accuracy.

Behavioral analytics is another technology gaining prominence in threat detection. By establishing baselines of normal user and system behavior, behavioral analytics tools can detect deviations that might indicate insider threats or compromised accounts. These solutions provide a dynamic approach to identifying risks.

Threat intelligence feeds are essential tools for staying informed about the latest threats and vulnerabilities.

Organizations subscribe to threat intelligence services that provide up-to-date information on known threats, attack vectors, and indicators of compromise (IoCs). Threat intelligence feeds help security teams proactively adjust their defenses and detection strategies.

Security orchestration, automation, and response (SOAR) platforms are designed to streamline and automate threat detection and response processes. They integrate with various security tools, enabling organizations to create workflows and playbooks for incident response. SOAR platforms enhance the efficiency of security teams and reduce response times.

Sandboxing technology is used to analyze potentially malicious files or code in an isolated environment. Sandboxes execute suspicious content in a controlled environment to determine whether it exhibits malicious behavior. This allows organizations to safely examine potential threats without risking their production systems.

Threat hunting is a proactive approach to threat detection that relies on the expertise of cybersecurity professionals. Threat hunters use various tools and techniques to search for signs of compromise or hidden threats within an organization's network. This human-driven approach complements automated detection technologies.

Deception technology involves creating decoy systems and assets within the network to lure attackers. When an attacker interacts with these decoys, security teams can detect their presence and intentions. Deception technology adds an additional layer of defense by actively engaging with potential threats.

Cloud-native security tools are essential for organizations that have adopted cloud computing. These tools are designed to monitor and protect cloud-based infrastructure and services. Cloud security posture management (CSPM) tools help organizations maintain secure configurations and compliance in the cloud.

Threat detection technologies are not standalone solutions; they work together in a layered defense strategy. Organizations typically employ a combination of these technologies, depending on their specific security requirements and the nature of their digital assets. The integration of these tools allows for a comprehensive and adaptive approach to threat detection.

To select the right technologies and tools for threat detection, organizations must consider their unique risk profile, industry regulations, and compliance requirements. Additionally, ongoing training and skill development for cybersecurity professionals are essential to effectively utilize these technologies and respond to emerging threats.

In summary, threat detection technologies and tools are vital components of a robust cybersecurity strategy. They encompass IDS, IPS, SIEM, EDR, machine learning, behavioral analytics, threat intelligence feeds, SOAR platforms, sandboxing, threat hunting, deception technology, and cloud-native security tools. By leveraging these technologies and integrating them into their security infrastructure, organizations can better protect themselves from a wide range of cyber threats and ensure the confidentiality, integrity, and availability of their digital assets.

Chapter 3: Building an Effective Security Operations Center (SOC)

Designing and setting up a Security Operations Center (SOC) is a critical step for organizations seeking to enhance their cybersecurity posture. A SOC serves as the nerve center for monitoring, detecting, and responding to security incidents, playing a pivotal role in safeguarding digital assets, sensitive data, and the overall integrity of the organization's operations.

The first and foremost consideration when designing a SOC is defining its objectives and scope. This involves determining what the SOC will protect, the types of threats it will focus on, and the specific assets or networks it will cover. Clarity in these areas is essential for creating an effective SOC strategy.

Next, selecting an appropriate SOC model is crucial. Organizations can choose between building an in-house SOC, outsourcing to a managed security service provider (MSSP), or adopting a hybrid approach that combines both internal and external resources. The choice depends on factors like budget, available expertise, and the organization's unique requirements.

Staffing the SOC with skilled professionals is paramount. A well-rounded SOC team typically includes security analysts, incident responders, threat hunters, and SOC managers. These individuals should possess a deep understanding of cybersecurity concepts, threat intelligence, and the tools and technologies used in the SOC.

Creating a SOC infrastructure involves selecting the right hardware, software, and security technologies. This includes the deployment of security information and event management (SIEM) systems, intrusion detection and prevention systems (IDS/IPS), endpoint detection and response (EDR) solutions, and threat intelligence feeds. Integrating these technologies ensures the SOC can effectively monitor and analyze security events.

Central to the SOC's effectiveness is the development of robust incident response procedures and playbooks. These documents detail the steps to follow when a security incident occurs, helping the team respond promptly and efficiently. Regularly testing and updating these procedures is vital to adapt to evolving threats.

In addition to technical tools and procedures, a SOC should have clear policies and guidelines for security monitoring and response. These policies outline the rules for accessing and handling sensitive data, incident escalation, communication protocols, and compliance with relevant regulations.

Continuous monitoring is a core function of the SOC. Security analysts and monitoring tools actively watch network traffic, log data, and other sources for indicators of compromise (IoCs) or abnormal activities. This real-time monitoring allows the SOC to detect potential threats as they emerge.

Threat intelligence plays a pivotal role in SOC operations. Access to up-to-date threat feeds and information on the latest vulnerabilities and attack vectors helps security analysts stay ahead of potential threats. Threat intelligence can be used to fine-tune monitoring and response strategies.

Effective communication and collaboration are essential within the SOC and with other parts of the organization. The SOC should establish communication channels and workflows to ensure seamless coordination during incident response. Regular reporting to executive leadership and stakeholders keeps them informed about the organization's security posture.

Automation and orchestration can significantly enhance SOC efficiency. Implementing automation for routine tasks, such as alert triage and incident classification, frees up analysts to focus on more complex threats. Orchestration allows for the integration of various security tools and technologies, streamlining response efforts.

Ensuring the resilience and redundancy of SOC operations is critical. Redundant data centers, backup power supplies, and disaster recovery plans should be in place to maintain SOC functionality in the face of unexpected disruptions or outages.

Compliance with relevant regulations and standards is a priority for many organizations. The SOC must align its activities with industry-specific requirements and international standards, such as GDPR, HIPAA, or ISO 27001. Compliance not only helps protect the organization from legal and financial risks but also demonstrates a commitment to security to clients and partners.

Ongoing training and skill development for SOC staff are imperative. Cyber threats are constantly evolving, and security professionals must stay updated with the latest trends and techniques. Continuous education and certifications, such as CISSP or CEH, can help keep SOC teams well-prepared.

Lastly, measuring and improving SOC performance is an ongoing process. Key performance indicators (KPIs) and metrics, such as mean time to detect (MTTD) and mean time to respond (MTTR), should be regularly monitored. Analyzing these metrics helps identify areas for improvement and adapt SOC strategies accordingly.

In summary, designing and setting up a SOC is a complex yet vital endeavor for organizations looking to protect their digital assets. It involves defining objectives, choosing the right SOC model, staffing with skilled professionals, deploying the necessary technologies, creating robust procedures, and maintaining compliance. Effective communication, automation, and continuous improvement are also essential elements in ensuring the SOC's success. As cyber threats continue to evolve, a well-designed and well-operated SOC is a critical component of any organization's cybersecurity strategy.

A Security Operations Center (SOC) is a pivotal element of an organization's cybersecurity strategy, but its effectiveness hinges on a well-structured workflow for incident handling. Understanding the SOC workflow and how it manages security incidents is essential for maintaining a strong security posture.

Incident Detection: The SOC workflow begins with the detection of security incidents. This involves continuous monitoring of various data sources, such as network traffic, system logs, and endpoint activity, to identify potential threats or abnormalities. The goal is to detect incidents as early as possible.

Alert Triage: Once an alert is generated, it undergoes triage. In this phase, security analysts assess the alert's validity and severity. Analysts determine whether the alert represents a genuine security incident or a false positive. False positives can consume valuable resources, so accurate triage is crucial.

Incident Classification: After triage, the SOC classifies the incident based on its nature and severity. Incidents are typically categorized as low, medium, or high severity, allowing the SOC to prioritize response efforts accordingly. Classification helps in resource allocation and response planning.

Initial Response: High-severity incidents demand immediate attention. The SOC initiates an initial response to mitigate the threat and minimize its impact. This response may involve isolating affected systems, blocking malicious traffic, or taking other immediate actions to contain the incident.

Incident Investigation: Simultaneously with the initial response, the SOC initiates an in-depth investigation. Security analysts gather additional information about the incident, such as the attacker's tactics, techniques, and procedures (TTPs), the scope of the compromise, and the potential impact on the organization.

Forensic Analysis: For certain incidents, especially those involving data breaches or sophisticated attacks, a forensic analysis may be necessary. This involves collecting and preserving digital evidence to understand the full extent of the incident, identify the attacker's entry point, and uncover any data exfiltration.

Communication and Escalation: Effective communication is vital throughout the SOC workflow. The SOC team must collaborate internally and with other stakeholders, including IT teams, legal, and executive leadership. Clear and timely communication ensures that everyone is informed about the incident's status and impact.

Incident Containment: Containing the incident is a critical step. The SOC works to prevent the attacker from further compromising systems or data. This may involve isolating affected systems, blocking specific IP addresses, or taking other measures to limit the attacker's access.

Eradication: After containment, the SOC focuses on eradicating the root cause of the incident. This might involve patching vulnerabilities, removing malware, or closing security gaps to prevent similar incidents in the future. Eradication ensures that the threat is fully removed from the environment.

Recovery: With the threat neutralized, the SOC can initiate the recovery phase. This involves restoring affected systems and services to their normal operation. The goal is to minimize downtime and resume business operations as swiftly as possible.

Documentation: Throughout the incident handling process, thorough documentation is crucial. SOC analysts record all actions taken, evidence collected, and decisions made. Proper documentation supports post-incident analysis, reporting, and compliance requirements.

Post-Incident Analysis: After the incident is resolved, the SOC conducts a post-incident analysis. This retrospective examination helps identify lessons learned, areas for improvement, and adjustments needed in security policies, procedures, or technologies.

Reporting: Reporting is a critical aspect of the SOC workflow. The SOC team creates detailed reports summarizing the incident, its impact, the response actions taken, and recommendations for preventing similar incidents in the future. These reports are shared with executive leadership and relevant stakeholders.

Incident Closure: The final phase of the SOC workflow is incident closure. This involves confirming that the incident has been fully resolved, all related actions have been completed, and the organization is back to normal operations. Closure signifies the end of the incident handling process.

Continuous Improvement: The SOC workflow is iterative. After each incident, the SOC team reviews its performance and identifies opportunities for improvement. This ongoing process of continuous improvement helps the SOC adapt to evolving threats and challenges.

In summary, the SOC workflow is a structured and dynamic process that guides the detection, response, and recovery from security incidents. It encompasses incident detection, alert triage, classification, response, investigation, communication, containment, eradication, recovery, documentation, analysis, reporting, closure, and continuous improvement. A well-executed SOC workflow is essential for safeguarding an organization's digital assets and maintaining a strong security posture in an ever-changing threat landscape.

Chapter 4: Threat Intelligence and Information Sharing

Gathering and analyzing threat intelligence is a crucial component of modern cybersecurity practices, allowing organizations to stay ahead of potential threats and vulnerabilities. Threat intelligence refers to information that helps organizations understand the tactics, techniques, and procedures (TTPs) of cyber adversaries, as well as the current threat landscape. In today's interconnected digital world, where cyber threats are constantly evolving, threat intelligence serves as a valuable tool for enhancing an organization's security posture.

Threat intelligence can come from various sources, including open-source intelligence (OSINT), closed-source intelligence (CSINT), and proprietary sources. OSINT includes publicly available information from websites, forums, social media, and news articles. CSINT, on the other hand, involves classified or confidential information obtained from government agencies or private cybersecurity firms. Proprietary sources are data collected and analyzed by commercial threat intelligence providers.

To gather threat intelligence effectively, organizations employ dedicated teams or tools that monitor and collect data from various sources. Automated tools can scrape websites and forums for mentions of known threats, vulnerabilities, or exploits, providing a constant stream of information. Additionally, organizations can subscribe to threat intelligence feeds and services that deliver timely updates on emerging threats and vulnerabilities specific to their industry or technology stack.

Once threat intelligence data is collected, it must be analyzed to extract meaningful insights. Analysts assess the credibility and relevance of the information and determine whether it poses a threat to their organization. To do this, they often rely on established frameworks and models, such as the Cyber Kill Chain or the Diamond Model, which help break down and understand the stages of a cyberattack and the associated indicators of compromise (IoCs).

Analyzing threat intelligence involves identifying patterns, trends, and anomalies in the data. Analysts look for commonalities in attack techniques, malware families, or targeted industries. They also pay attention to the tactics used by threat actors, such as phishing, ransomware, or advanced persistent threats (APTs). The goal is to gain a deeper understanding of the threats facing the organization, allowing for better preparedness and response.

One key aspect of threat intelligence analysis is attribution, which involves identifying the threat actor responsible for a specific attack or campaign. Attribution can be challenging, as threat actors often take steps to hide their identity and location. However, by examining various indicators, such as the malware used, the infrastructure employed, or the language and cultural references in attack messages, analysts can sometimes make educated guesses about the origin of the threat.

Effective threat intelligence analysis goes beyond just identifying threats. It also helps organizations assess the potential impact of those threats on their specific environment. Analysts consider factors like the organization's technology stack, network architecture, and existing security controls to determine the likelihood of a successful attack and the potential damage it could cause.

Another critical aspect of threat intelligence analysis is the dissemination of actionable intelligence to the appropriate teams within an organization. This ensures that the insights gained from threat intelligence are used to enhance security measures effectively. For example, if a threat intelligence report identifies a specific vulnerability in a widely used software application, the organization's vulnerability management team can prioritize patching or mitigation efforts.

Sharing threat intelligence is not limited to within an organization; many industries and sectors have established Information Sharing and Analysis Centers (ISACs) or Information Sharing and Analysis Organizations (ISAOs) that facilitate the sharing of threat intelligence among member organizations. This collaborative approach helps create a more comprehensive view of the threat landscape and allows organizations to learn from each other's experiences.

Additionally, governments and law enforcement agencies often share threat intelligence with private-sector organizations to help protect critical infrastructure and national security interests. These partnerships can be especially valuable when dealing with nation-state actors and large-scale cyber threats.

While gathering and analyzing threat intelligence is essential, it's equally important to ensure that the intelligence is actionable. This means that organizations need to have well-defined incident response plans and procedures in place to act upon the intelligence received. Threat intelligence is most valuable when it leads to proactive measures that enhance security, such as patching vulnerabilities, updating security policies, or improving employee training.

In summary, gathering and analyzing threat intelligence is a fundamental aspect of modern cybersecurity. It empowers organizations to understand the evolving threat landscape, identify potential risks, and take proactive measures to protect their digital assets. By effectively collecting, analyzing, and disseminating threat intelligence, organizations can enhance their cybersecurity posture and stay one step ahead of cyber adversaries in an increasingly complex and interconnected digital world. Collaborative threat information sharing is a vital practice in the realm of cybersecurity, enabling organizations to work together in addressing the ever-evolving landscape of cyber threats. In today's interconnected digital world, where cyberattacks are becoming more sophisticated and frequent, no single organization can defend against all potential threats alone. Collaborative threat information sharing involves the exchange of information, insights, and intelligence related to cyber threats, vulnerabilities, and attack tactics among various entities, including private-sector organizations, government agencies, cybersecurity firms, and research institutions. This cooperative approach allows participating organizations to leverage collective knowledge and resources to better protect themselves against cyber threats. One of the primary motivations for collaborative threat information sharing is the recognition that threat actors often target multiple organizations across different sectors. When one organization experiences a cyber incident, the information about the attack can be invaluable to others who may face a similar threat. Sharing this information can help prevent other potential victims from falling prey to the same attack.

Collaborative sharing can take various forms, including the exchange of threat intelligence reports, indicators of compromise (IoCs), attack patterns, and even detailed technical analysis of malware or attack infrastructure. Such information sharing can occur through formalized frameworks and organizations or through informal networks and trusted relationships.

One notable example of formalized information sharing is the establishment of Information Sharing and Analysis Centers (ISACs) and Information Sharing and Analysis Organizations (ISAOs). These organizations serve as hubs for collecting, analyzing, and disseminating threat information among their member organizations within specific industries or sectors.

ISACs and ISAOs cover a wide range of industries, including financial services, healthcare, energy, and more. They play a pivotal role in connecting organizations that may not have direct relationships but share common threats and interests within their sector.

Government agencies, such as the Department of Homeland Security (DHS) in the United States, often work closely with ISACs and ISAOs to facilitate the sharing of threat intelligence between the public and private sectors. This collaboration is particularly important when addressing threats to critical infrastructure.

Collaborative threat information sharing also extends to the global stage, with international organizations and alliances, such as the Forum of Incident Response and Security Teams (FIRST) and the Cyber Threat Alliance (CTA). These organizations facilitate cross-border cooperation in sharing cyber threat information and jointly addressing cybercrime and cyber espionage activities. Additionally, the private sector actively participates in collaborative sharing through industry-specific groups and forums. Technology companies, for instance, often collaborate to identify and counter emerging threats. When a new software vulnerability is discovered, responsible disclosure practices ensure that information about the vulnerability is shared with the affected vendor so that they can develop patches and mitigate the risk. The benefits of collaborative threat information sharing are numerous. First and foremost, it allows organizations to enhance their situational awareness by staying informed about the latest threats and vulnerabilities. This, in turn, enables them to better prioritize their cybersecurity efforts and allocate resources where they are needed most.

Moreover, collaborative sharing helps organizations detect threats earlier in the attack lifecycle. When one organization identifies an indicator of compromise or a novel attack technique, it can share this information with others, allowing them to proactively adjust their defenses and monitoring strategies.

Another significant advantage of collaborative sharing is the ability to pool resources and expertise. Organizations with limited cybersecurity resources can benefit from the collective knowledge and capabilities of a larger community. This can include access to specialized threat intelligence feeds, threat hunting tools, and incident response expertise.

Furthermore, collaborative threat information sharing supports a more effective incident response. In the event of a security breach or cyber incident, organizations can quickly access relevant threat intelligence and guidance from trusted sources, expediting their efforts to contain and remediate the incident.

Despite its many advantages, collaborative threat information sharing is not without its challenges. One of the primary concerns among organizations is the sharing of sensitive or proprietary information. To address this, sharing mechanisms often allow for the anonymization and aggregation of data to protect the privacy and confidentiality of participating entities.

Trust is another critical factor in successful collaborative sharing. Organizations must have confidence in the security and integrity of the sharing platform or network. Establishing trust among participants often requires the development of legal agreements, standard operating procedures, and robust data protection measures.

Additionally, there may be legal and regulatory hurdles to overcome when sharing threat information across borders. Different countries have varying laws and regulations governing data sharing and privacy, which can complicate international collaboration efforts.

In summary, collaborative threat information sharing is an essential practice in modern cybersecurity. It enables organizations to collectively defend against cyber threats that no single entity could address effectively alone. By participating in formalized organizations, informal networks, and industry-specific groups, organizations can enhance their cybersecurity posture and contribute to the broader goal of creating a safer digital environment for all.

Chapter 5: Leveraging Metasploit for Blue Team Operations

Metasploit, a powerful and versatile penetration testing framework, is often associated with offensive cybersecurity activities, including vulnerability assessment and exploit development. However, it can also be a valuable tool for organizations when used for defensive purposes and enhancing overall cybersecurity resilience.

One of the primary ways Metasploit can be employed defensively is for vulnerability assessment and management. By simulating attacks against their own systems, organizations can identify weaknesses and vulnerabilities before malicious actors can exploit them. This proactive approach allows for timely patching and remediation, reducing the risk of successful cyberattacks.

Metasploit's scanning and auditing capabilities enable organizations to conduct regular vulnerability assessments. This includes identifying open ports, services, and potential weaknesses in their network infrastructure. By regularly scanning and assessing their systems, organizations can maintain an up-to-date inventory of assets and ensure they are properly secured.

Additionally, Metasploit provides valuable insights into the severity and potential impact of vulnerabilities. Security teams can prioritize remediation efforts based on the criticality of each vulnerability and its potential impact on the organization's operations.

Metasploit also allows for the validation of patches and fixes. Before deploying updates to production systems, organizations can use Metasploit to confirm that the applied patches effectively mitigate the identified vulnerabilities. This validation process helps prevent potential disruptions and ensures that the patches are indeed addressing the issues.

Furthermore, Metasploit can be used to test the effectiveness of security controls and monitoring systems. By simulating attacks and evasion techniques, organizations can assess their security posture and identify gaps in their defenses. This proactive approach helps organizations strengthen their security measures and refine incident response plans.

Another defensive use of Metasploit is in the realm of red teaming and adversary emulation. Red teaming involves simulating realistic cyberattacks to evaluate an organization's readiness and response capabilities. Metasploit can serve as a valuable tool for red teamers, allowing them to emulate real-world threats and tactics to assess an organization's defenses comprehensively.

Red teaming exercises using Metasploit can help organizations identify weaknesses in their security operations, incident response procedures, and employee awareness. These insights enable organizations to make informed improvements to their cybersecurity strategies and enhance their ability to detect, respond to, and mitigate threats effectively.

Metasploit can also play a role in threat hunting and proactive threat detection. Security teams can use the framework to conduct searches for specific indicators of compromise (IoCs) or unusual behavior within their network environments. This approach helps organizations detect and respond to potential threats in their early stages, reducing the dwell time of attackers within their networks.

Moreover, Metasploit can be used to assess the security of web applications and services. Organizations can conduct simulated attacks, such as SQL injection or cross-site scripting (XSS) tests, to identify vulnerabilities in their web assets. This proactive testing approach enables organizations to address issues before they can be exploited by malicious actors.

Metasploit's versatility extends to assessing the security of IoT (Internet of Things) devices. With the proliferation of IoT devices in both consumer and enterprise environments, organizations can use Metasploit to evaluate the security posture of these devices, identifying potential entry points for attackers.

To use Metasploit for defensive purposes effectively, organizations should invest in training and education for their cybersecurity teams. Understanding the framework's capabilities and how to leverage them for defensive tasks is crucial. Additionally, organizations should consider incorporating Metasploit into their overall cybersecurity strategy and integrating it with other security tools and processes.

In summary, Metasploit, known for its offensive capabilities, can be harnessed for defensive purposes as well. Organizations can use it for vulnerability assessment, security validation, red teaming, threat hunting, and assessing the security of web applications and IoT devices. When used as part of a comprehensive cybersecurity strategy, Metasploit contributes to strengthening an organization's defenses and overall resilience in the face of evolving cyber threats.

As we delve into the realm of cybersecurity and the strategies employed by blue teams, it's important to understand that the landscape of digital threats is constantly evolving. Blue teams, comprising the defenders of digital infrastructure and data, play a crucial role in safeguarding organizations against cyberattacks. Next, we'll explore how blue teams can leverage the power of Metasploit, traditionally seen as a tool for red teams and penetration testers, to bolster their defensive capabilities.

Metasploit, originally designed for offensive security tasks, has evolved over the years to become a versatile platform that can be used by blue teams as well. When it comes to defending against cyber threats, knowledge is power. Blue teams can use Metasploit to gain insights into the same vulnerabilities and attack vectors that malicious actors might target.

One of the key advantages of Metasploit for blue teams is its vulnerability scanning and assessment capabilities. By utilizing Metasploit's scanning modules, blue teams can proactively identify weaknesses within their organization's network and systems. This allows them to prioritize vulnerabilities based on severity and potential impact, ensuring that critical issues are addressed first.

Metasploit's scanning features also enable blue teams to keep an up-to-date inventory of their assets and configurations. This knowledge is essential for maintaining a strong security posture and responding swiftly to potential threats.

Beyond scanning, Metasploit provides blue teams with the tools to validate patches and security fixes. Before deploying updates to production systems, organizations can use Metasploit to verify that the patches effectively mitigate the identified vulnerabilities. This validation process helps prevent potential disruptions and ensures that the applied fixes are robust.

Furthermore, Metasploit can assist blue teams in testing the effectiveness of their security controls and monitoring systems. By simulating attacks and evasion techniques, they can assess the resilience of their defenses. This proactive approach enables organizations to fine-tune their security measures and enhance their ability to detect, respond to, and mitigate threats effectively.

Blue teams can also use Metasploit for threat hunting and proactive threat detection. The platform allows them to conduct searches for specific indicators of compromise (IoCs) or unusual behavior within their network environments. This approach helps organizations detect and respond to potential threats in their early stages, minimizing the time adversaries have within their networks.

Metasploit can play a vital role in incident response as well. In the event of a security incident, blue teams can use the platform to simulate and analyze the attack scenario, helping them understand the extent of the breach and how it occurred. This knowledge is invaluable for developing effective containment and remediation strategies.

Moreover, Metasploit's versatility extends to the realm of web application security. Blue teams can employ it to assess the security of their web assets by conducting simulated attacks, such as SQL injection or cross-site scripting (XSS) tests. Identifying and addressing vulnerabilities in web applications is crucial, as they are common targets for attackers.

Metasploit's capabilities also encompass the assessment of IoT (Internet of Things) device security. With the growing prevalence of IoT devices, organizations can use Metasploit to evaluate the security posture of these devices and identify potential risks associated with their use.

To effectively leverage Metasploit as a blue team, organizations should invest in training and education for their cybersecurity professionals. Understanding the platform's capabilities and how to use them for defensive purposes is paramount. Integrating Metasploit into an organization's overall cybersecurity strategy and aligning it with other security tools and processes enhances its effectiveness.

In summary, Metasploit, a tool traditionally associated with offensive security, has valuable applications for blue teams as well. Its scanning, vulnerability assessment, security validation, and threat detection capabilities empower blue teams to proactively defend against cyber threats. When used strategically, Metasploit can be a potent asset in the arsenal of defenders, contributing to a robust cybersecurity posture and the protection of digital assets.

Chapter 6: Advanced Incident Detection Techniques

In the ever-evolving landscape of cybersecurity, advanced threat detection methods have become a critical component of any organization's defense strategy. These methods are essential for identifying and mitigating sophisticated threats that often bypass traditional security measures.

One of the key aspects of advanced threat detection is the shift from signature-based detection to behavior-based and anomaly detection. Signature-based approaches rely on known patterns and signatures of malware or attacks. While effective against known threats, they struggle to detect novel and evolving attack techniques.

Behavior-based detection, on the other hand, focuses on monitoring the behavior of systems, users, and network traffic. This approach looks for deviations from established baselines. For example, if a user who typically accesses only HR files suddenly attempts to access sensitive financial data, it could trigger an alert. This behavior-based approach is more adaptive and can detect previously unknown threats based on their unusual activities.

Machine learning and artificial intelligence (AI) play a significant role in advanced threat detection. These technologies enable security systems to analyze massive amounts of data and identify subtle patterns or anomalies that may indicate an attack. Machine learning algorithms can be trained on historical data to recognize normal behavior and subsequently detect deviations from it.

User and entity behavior analytics (UEBA) is a subset of advanced threat detection that focuses on user and entity activities within an organization. UEBA systems can analyze user behavior, such as login times, locations, and the applications they access. When a user's behavior deviates significantly from their historical patterns or established norms, the system can generate alerts for further investigation.

Threat intelligence feeds and information sharing have become crucial in advanced threat detection. Organizations can subscribe to threat intelligence services that provide real-time information about emerging threats and vulnerabilities. This data helps security teams stay informed about the current threat landscape and adapt their defenses accordingly.

Another important aspect of advanced threat detection is the integration of multiple security tools and data sources. Organizations can leverage security information and event management (SIEM) systems to collect and correlate data from various sources, such as firewalls, antivirus software, intrusion detection systems, and more. This centralized approach allows for more comprehensive threat detection and response.

Sandboxing is a technique used in advanced threat detection to analyze potentially malicious files or code in an isolated environment. When a suspicious file or attachment is detected, it is executed within a sandbox to observe its behavior. If the behavior is indicative of malicious intent, the file is flagged as a threat.

Endpoint detection and response (EDR) solutions are designed to monitor and respond to threats at the endpoint level, such as individual devices or servers. EDR solutions can provide visibility into endpoint activities, detect suspicious behavior, and enable rapid incident response.

Threat hunting is a proactive approach to advanced threat detection where security analysts actively search for signs of compromise within an organization's network. This involves investigating logs, network traffic, and endpoint data to identify threats that may have gone undetected by automated systems.

Deception technology is an emerging field in advanced threat detection. It involves deploying decoy systems, data, or credentials to lure attackers into revealing their presence. Deception technology can help organizations detect threats at an early stage and gain insights into attackers' tactics, techniques, and procedures.

Continuous monitoring and real-time analysis are fundamental to advanced threat detection. Security teams must be vigilant in monitoring network traffic, system logs, and user activities for any signs of suspicious behavior. Real-time analysis can help organizations respond to threats as they unfold, minimizing potential damage.

Intrusion detection and prevention systems (IDPS) are essential components of advanced threat detection. These systems monitor network traffic for signs of unauthorized access or malicious activity. IDPS can automatically block or mitigate threats in real-time.

Cloud-based security solutions are increasingly adopted for advanced threat detection, especially as organizations migrate to cloud environments. Cloud-based solutions offer scalability and flexibility, allowing organizations to adapt to changing threat landscapes.

In summary, advanced threat detection methods are essential in today's cybersecurity landscape. Signature-based detection alone is no longer sufficient to protect organizations from evolving threats. By embracing behavior-based detection, machine learning, threat intelligence, integration of security tools, sandboxing, EDR, threat hunting, deception technology, continuous monitoring, and cloud-based solutions, organizations can significantly enhance their ability to detect and respond to advanced threats. As cyber adversaries become more sophisticated, the importance of advanced threat detection methods cannot be overstated in maintaining the security and integrity of digital assets.

Behavioral and anomaly-based detection are two critical approaches in modern cybersecurity, aimed at identifying and mitigating threats that evade traditional security measures. These methods represent a paradigm shift from signature-based detection to a more adaptive, proactive, and dynamic approach to cybersecurity.

In the world of cybersecurity, attackers are constantly evolving their tactics to bypass conventional security defenses. Traditional signature-based detection relies on known patterns and signatures of malware or attacks. While effective at recognizing previously identified threats, it often struggles to detect novel and emerging threats, which do not have well-defined signatures.

This is where behavioral and anomaly-based detection steps in. Instead of relying on known signatures, these approaches focus on monitoring and analyzing the behavior of systems, users, and network traffic. By doing so, they can detect deviations from established baselines or norms, even when dealing with previously unseen threats.

Imagine a scenario where an organization's network typically experiences a consistent pattern of user behavior. Suddenly, one day, a user who typically accesses only HR-related files begins attempting to access sensitive financial data. This unusual behavior could trigger an alert in a behavioral detection system, indicating a potential security breach.

Machine learning and artificial intelligence (AI) are integral to the success of behavioral and anomaly-based detection. These technologies enable security systems to analyze vast amounts of data, identify subtle patterns, and detect anomalies that might indicate an attack. Machine learning algorithms can be trained on historical data to recognize normal behavior, allowing them to spot deviations efficiently.

User and entity behavior analytics (UEBA) is a subset of behavioral detection that concentrates on user and entity activities within an organization. UEBA systems continuously analyze user behavior, such as login times, locations, applications accessed, and data accessed. When a user's behavior significantly deviates from their historical patterns or established norms, the UEBA system generates alerts for further investigation.

The power of these detection methods lies in their adaptability and their ability to evolve with the threat landscape. Unlike static signatures, which can become obsolete as attackers modify their tactics, behavioral and anomaly-based detection can adapt to new attack vectors and techniques.

To facilitate these adaptive methods, organizations are increasingly leveraging threat intelligence feeds and information sharing. Threat intelligence services provide real-time data on emerging threats and vulnerabilities, helping security teams stay informed about the evolving threat landscape and adjust their defenses accordingly.

Another critical aspect of behavioral and anomaly-based detection is the integration of multiple security tools and data sources. Organizations employ security information and event management (SIEM) systems to collect and correlate data from various sources, such as firewalls, antivirus software, intrusion detection systems, and more. This centralized approach enables a more comprehensive understanding of the threat landscape.

In advanced threat detection, sandboxing plays a vital role. When a suspicious file or attachment is detected, it is executed within a sandboxed environment that isolates it from the production network. This allows security teams to observe its behavior without risking a compromise of the entire network. If the behavior exhibited within the sandbox is indicative of malicious intent, the file is flagged as a threat. Endpoint detection and response (EDR) solutions are designed to monitor and respond to threats at the endpoint level. These endpoints can be individual devices or servers within an organization's network. EDR solutions provide visibility into endpoint activities, detect suspicious behavior, and enable rapid incident response, helping to contain threats before they can spread.

Behavioral and anomaly-based detection also encompass the practice of threat hunting. This proactive approach involves security analysts actively searching for signs of compromise within an organization's network. Analysts investigate logs, network traffic, and endpoint data to identify threats that may have eluded automated detection systems.

Deception technology is an emerging field within this realm. It involves deploying decoy systems, data, or credentials to lure attackers into revealing their presence. Deception technology can help organizations detect threats at an early stage and gain insights into attackers' tactics, techniques, and procedures.

In the world of continuous monitoring and real-time analysis, security teams must remain vigilant. They monitor network traffic, system logs, and user activities for any signs of suspicious behavior. Real-time analysis can help organizations respond to threats as they unfold, minimizing potential damage and exposure.

Intrusion detection and prevention systems (IDPS) are foundational components of behavioral and anomaly-based detection. These systems continuously monitor network traffic for signs of unauthorized access or malicious activity.

When a potential threat is detected, IDPS can automatically block or mitigate it in real-time.

As organizations increasingly migrate to cloud environments, cloud-based security solutions are playing a more prominent role in advanced threat detection. These solutions offer scalability and flexibility, allowing organizations to adapt to changing threat landscapes while securing their cloud assets.

In summary, behavioral and anomaly-based detection are at the forefront of modern cybersecurity. They represent a shift from traditional signature-based methods to a more adaptive, proactive, and dynamic approach. By leveraging behavioral analysis, machine learning, threat intelligence, integration of security tools, sandboxing, EDR, threat hunting, deception technology, continuous monitoring, and cloud-based solutions, organizations can significantly enhance their ability to detect and respond to advanced threats. In a world where cyber adversaries continuously evolve their tactics, the importance of these methods cannot be overstated in maintaining the security and integrity of digital assets.

Chapter 7: Threat Hunting with Metasploit

Proactive threat hunting is a crucial cybersecurity practice that aims to identify and mitigate security threats before they can cause significant harm to an organization's digital assets and data. Unlike traditional security approaches that rely primarily on reactive measures, such as signature-based detection and incident response, proactive threat hunting is about taking a more active and anticipatory stance in safeguarding against cyber threats.

In today's complex and rapidly evolving threat landscape, cyber adversaries are continually developing new tactics, techniques, and procedures (TTPs) to evade detection and infiltrate networks. While reactive measures are necessary for addressing known threats, they often fall short in detecting sophisticated, zero-day, or targeted attacks that don't have readily available signatures or indicators of compromise.

Proactive threat hunting acknowledges the limitations of reactive security measures and seeks to bridge the gap by actively searching for signs of compromise within an organization's network and systems. It involves a systematic and continuous effort to uncover hidden threats and vulnerabilities, often using a combination of human expertise, advanced analytics, and threat intelligence.

One of the fundamental principles of proactive threat hunting is the assumption that attackers are already present within the network, even if their presence has not yet been detected. This assumption encourages security teams to adopt a mindset of skepticism and thorough investigation, ensuring that no stone is left unturned when looking for potential threats.

Proactive threat hunting can take various forms, but it generally involves the following key elements:

Data Collection and Analysis: Security teams gather vast amounts of data from diverse sources within the organization's environment, including network traffic logs, endpoint telemetry, system logs, and application data. This data is then analyzed to identify patterns, anomalies, and potential indicators of compromise.

Threat Intelligence Integration: Threat intelligence feeds and sources play a critical role in proactive threat hunting. They provide valuable information about emerging threats, attacker tactics, and known attack infrastructure. Integrating threat intelligence into the hunting process helps security teams stay informed and focused on relevant threats.

Hypothesis-Driven Investigation: Proactive threat hunting often begins with forming hypotheses based on known attacker behaviors, tactics, or vulnerabilities. Security analysts develop these hypotheses to guide their investigations and searches for potential threats. For example, a hypothesis might involve searching for signs of lateral movement within the network.

Behavioral Analysis: Behavioral analysis is a central component of proactive threat hunting. It involves monitoring and analyzing the behavior of systems, users, and network traffic. Security teams look for deviations from established baselines or norms, as these deviations can indicate potential threats. For instance, a sudden increase in outbound network traffic from an employee's workstation could raise suspicion.

Endpoint and Network Telemetry: Proactive threat hunting often leverages endpoint detection and response (EDR) solutions and intrusion detection systems to gather telemetry data. This data provides visibility into endpoint activities, enabling security teams to spot unusual or suspicious behavior at the endpoint level.

Incident Response Practices: While proactive threat hunting focuses on detecting threats early, it is closely tied to incident response. When potential threats are identified, they must be thoroughly investigated, and appropriate actions taken to remediate and contain the threat. This requires well-defined incident response processes.

Continuous Improvement: Proactive threat hunting is an ongoing process that requires continuous improvement and adaptation. Security teams must learn from their hunting activities and adjust their strategies based on the evolving threat landscape.

It's important to note that proactive threat hunting is a resource-intensive activity that relies heavily on skilled security analysts and advanced tools and technologies. Organizations may choose to build in-house threat hunting teams or seek assistance from managed security service providers (MSSPs) with expertise in proactive threat hunting. Ultimately, proactive threat hunting is a proactive and strategic approach to cybersecurity that aims to stay ahead of cyber threats by actively seeking them out within an organization's environment. By complementing traditional security measures with proactive hunting practices, organizations can increase their chances of detecting and mitigating threats before they lead to data breaches or other security incidents. In a world where cyber threats continue to evolve in sophistication and scale, proactive threat hunting is a crucial component of a robust cybersecurity strategy.

Threat hunting techniques using Metasploit, an open-source penetration testing and vulnerability assessment tool, offer a powerful way to proactively identify and remediate security vulnerabilities and threats within an organization's network and systems. While Metasploit is often associated with offensive security and penetration testing, it can also be a valuable asset for defenders seeking to improve their security posture and stay one step ahead of cyber adversaries.

Metasploit is a versatile framework that provides a wide range of capabilities for conducting security assessments and penetration tests. However, it can also be harnessed as a threat hunting tool to identify and address vulnerabilities before they are exploited by malicious actors. This chapter explores various threat hunting techniques using Metasploit and how security teams can leverage this tool effectively.

Vulnerability Scanning and Assessment: Metasploit can be used to scan networks and systems for known vulnerabilities. Security professionals can launch scans and identify weaknesses in their environment that attackers could exploit. By proactively addressing these vulnerabilities, organizations reduce their attack surface and enhance their security posture.

Exploiting Known Vulnerabilities: Threat hunters can use Metasploit to exploit known vulnerabilities within their network, simulating potential attacks. By exploiting these vulnerabilities in a controlled environment, security teams gain valuable insights into potential risks and weaknesses that need immediate attention.

Credential Enumeration: One common tactic employed by threat actors is credential theft and abuse. Metasploit can be used to enumerate and test credentials within an organization's network. This technique helps identify weak or reused passwords that may be targeted by attackers.

Pivoting and Lateral Movement: In the context of threat hunting, Metasploit can be used to simulate lateral movement within the network. By moving laterally between compromised systems, security teams can identify potential paths that attackers might take to escalate their access and reach critical assets.

Port Scanning and Service Enumeration: Metasploit can conduct port scans and service enumeration to identify open ports and running services on networked devices. This information is critical for detecting potential vulnerabilities and misconfigurations.

Payload Generation and Execution: Metasploit allows for the creation of custom payloads that can be used to simulate attacks on vulnerable systems. Security professionals can execute these payloads to assess the effectiveness of their security controls and identify weaknesses.

Integration with Threat Intelligence: Threat hunters can integrate threat intelligence feeds and indicators of compromise (IOCs) into Metasploit. This integration enables the tool to actively search for signs of known threats or malicious activity within the organization's network.

Custom Module Development: Metasploit's modular architecture allows security teams to create custom modules tailored to their specific threat hunting needs. These modules can be used to test for unique vulnerabilities or configurations that are relevant to the organization.

Scenario-Based Simulations: Threat hunters can create scenario-based simulations in Metasploit to mimic specific threat scenarios. For example, they can simulate a phishing attack and track how it propagates through the network.

Comprehensive Reporting: Metasploit provides reporting capabilities that allow security teams to document their findings and observations during threat hunting exercises. These reports can be used to communicate vulnerabilities and recommended remediation steps to relevant stakeholders.

Continuous Monitoring: Threat hunting is an ongoing process, and Metasploit can be leveraged for continuous monitoring of the network. Regular scans and assessments help security teams stay vigilant and ensure that new vulnerabilities are promptly identified and addressed.

Red and Blue Teaming: Organizations can use Metasploit in red teaming exercises, where internal or external teams simulate attacks to test the organization's defenses. Conversely, blue teaming exercises use Metasploit to defend against simulated attacks and strengthen security controls.

In summary, Metasploit is a versatile tool that can be used for both offensive and defensive security purposes. When employed as part of a threat hunting strategy, it empowers security teams to actively seek out vulnerabilities and threats within their environment. By using Metasploit's features and capabilities effectively, organizations can proactively address weaknesses, enhance their security posture, and better protect their critical assets from cyber threats. Threat hunting with Metasploit is an essential component of a proactive and robust cybersecurity strategy.

Chapter 8: Incident Response and Mitigation

Incident response procedures are a critical component of any organization's cybersecurity strategy, serving as the blueprint for how the organization will react when a security incident occurs. These procedures are designed to minimize damage, reduce recovery time, and ultimately, protect the organization's data and assets. Next, we will explore the key elements of effective incident response procedures and how organizations can develop and implement them.

Preparation is Key: Effective incident response starts with thorough preparation. Organizations must identify potential threats and vulnerabilities, assess their risk, and develop strategies for mitigating these risks. This includes creating an incident response team, defining their roles and responsibilities, and ensuring they have the necessary training and resources.

Clearly Defined Incident Categories: To streamline incident response efforts, organizations should establish clear categories for different types of incidents. These categories help responders quickly identify the nature and severity of an incident and initiate the appropriate response procedures.

Incident Identification: The first step in responding to a security incident is identifying that an incident has occurred. This can be done through various means, such as automated monitoring tools, employee reports, or third-party notifications. Having clear processes for reporting and escalating incidents is essential.

Initial Assessment: Once an incident is identified, the incident response team must conduct an initial assessment to determine the scope and impact of the incident. This includes gathering relevant information, assessing the criticality of affected systems, and understanding potential risks to data and operations.

Containment: After the initial assessment, the focus shifts to containment. The goal is to prevent further damage and limit the incident's impact. This may involve isolating affected systems, disabling compromised accounts, or blocking malicious network traffic.

Eradication: Once containment is achieved, organizations must work to eradicate the root cause of the incident. This often involves removing malware, closing vulnerabilities, and implementing security patches or updates.

Recovery: With the threat eliminated, the organization can begin the recovery process. This involves restoring affected systems and services to their normal state. Backups play a crucial role in the recovery phase, allowing organizations to roll back to a known good state.

Communication: Effective communication is vital during an incident. Organizations must establish clear lines of communication within the incident response team and with external stakeholders, such as customers, partners, and law enforcement agencies. Transparency and timely updates build trust and help manage the incident's impact.

Documentation: Throughout the incident response process, detailed documentation is essential. This includes records of actions taken, evidence collected, and lessons learned. Documentation serves not only as a historical record but also as a valuable resource for post-incident analysis and improvement.

Legal and Regulatory Compliance: Organizations must be mindful of legal and regulatory requirements when responding to security incidents. Depending on the nature of the incident, there may be reporting obligations, privacy considerations, and legal implications that must be addressed.

Continuous Improvement: Effective incident response procedures are not static. They should be subject to regular review and improvement. After each incident, organizations should conduct a post-incident analysis to identify weaknesses in their response and make necessary adjustments.

Training and Awareness: Incident response is a team effort, and all employees should be aware of their role in the process. Regular training and awareness programs ensure that employees can recognize and report incidents promptly.

External Partnerships: Organizations can benefit from partnerships with external entities, such as incident response firms, cybersecurity information-sharing organizations, and law enforcement agencies. These partnerships provide access to expertise, threat intelligence, and additional resources.

Tabletop Exercises: To test the effectiveness of their incident response procedures, organizations can conduct tabletop exercises. These simulated scenarios help teams practice their response and identify areas that need improvement.

Cyber Insurance: Many organizations invest in cyber insurance to help cover the financial costs associated with security incidents. Understanding the terms and coverage of cyber insurance policies is essential for an effective response.

Crisis Communication: In some incidents, particularly those involving data breaches, crisis communication becomes a significant component of the response. Organizations should have a well-defined crisis communication plan in place.

Cultural Considerations: Developing a security-conscious organizational culture is essential for effective incident response. Employees at all levels should prioritize security and understand the role they play in incident prevention and response.

In summary, effective incident response procedures are a cornerstone of cybersecurity. They help organizations mitigate the impact of security incidents, reduce recovery time, and safeguard their data and assets. By following a well-defined incident response plan, organizations can ensure a swift and coordinated response to security incidents, ultimately strengthening their overall cybersecurity posture.

Mitigating and recovering from security incidents is a critical aspect of cybersecurity that organizations must prioritize in today's threat landscape. When an incident occurs, swift and effective action can make a significant difference in minimizing damage and reducing downtime. Next, we will delve into strategies and best practices for mitigating and recovering from security incidents.

The first step in mitigating and recovering from a security incident is to establish an incident response plan. This plan outlines the processes and procedures that the organization will follow when a security incident is detected. It should define the roles and responsibilities of the incident response team, including who will be responsible for coordinating the response, gathering evidence, communicating with stakeholders, and making critical decisions.

Once an incident response plan is in place, it's essential to continuously monitor the organization's environment for signs of suspicious or malicious activity. Early detection is crucial because it allows the organization to respond quickly and potentially prevent the incident from escalating. This monitoring can include the use of intrusion detection systems, security information and event management (SIEM) solutions, and threat intelligence feeds.

When an incident is detected, the incident response team must spring into action. The first priority is containment. Containment involves isolating the affected systems or networks to prevent further damage or unauthorized access. This may involve disconnecting compromised servers from the network, blocking malicious network traffic, or disabling compromised user accounts.

Simultaneously, it's essential to gather evidence related to the incident. This evidence may be crucial for understanding the nature of the attack, identifying the threat actor, and potentially pursuing legal actions. The incident response team should follow established procedures for preserving and collecting evidence, ensuring that it remains admissible in legal proceedings if necessary.

With containment in place and evidence collected, the organization can proceed to eradicate the root cause of the incident. This often involves removing malware, closing vulnerabilities, and patching or updating affected systems. Eradication is a critical step in preventing future incidents of the same nature.

The recovery phase focuses on restoring affected systems and services to their normal state. Backups play a significant role in this phase, as they allow organizations to roll back to a known good state before the incident occurred. Ensuring that backups are regularly tested and up-to-date is essential for an effective recovery process.

Communication is paramount throughout the incident response process. Organizations must maintain clear and transparent communication with internal and external stakeholders. This includes notifying senior management, legal counsel, law enforcement agencies (if necessary), and affected customers or partners. Transparency in communication helps manage the incident's impact and maintain trust.

Legal and regulatory considerations often come into play during incident mitigation and recovery. Depending on the nature of the incident and the organization's industry, there may be reporting obligations to regulatory authorities or data breach notification requirements to affected individuals. Legal counsel should be consulted to ensure compliance with relevant laws and regulations.

It's essential to engage with external resources when necessary. Organizations can benefit from partnering with incident response firms, cybersecurity information-sharing organizations, and law enforcement agencies. These partnerships provide access to expertise, threat intelligence, and additional resources that can enhance the incident response effort.

During the recovery phase, organizations should conduct a thorough post-incident analysis. This analysis involves reviewing the incident response process, identifying areas for improvement, and updating the incident response plan accordingly. Lessons learned from one incident can help strengthen the organization's security posture and preparedness for future incidents.

In addition to addressing the technical aspects of incident mitigation and recovery, organizations should also consider the human element. Employees play a critical role in both preventing and responding to incidents. Regular training and awareness programs help employees recognize and report security incidents promptly. A security-conscious organizational culture fosters a sense of responsibility for cybersecurity at all levels.

Incident recovery is not just about technical remediation; it also involves managing the organization's reputation and public image. A well-defined crisis communication plan is essential for handling incidents, especially those involving data breaches. Organizations should be prepared to communicate with affected individuals and the public, providing accurate information and addressing concerns.

Cyber insurance can also play a role in mitigating the financial impact of security incidents. Organizations should understand the terms and coverage of their cyber insurance policies and be prepared to engage with their insurance providers as needed during incident recovery.

In summary, mitigating and recovering from security incidents requires a well-structured and coordinated approach. Organizations must have an incident response plan in place, prioritize early detection, and take swift action to contain and eradicate threats. Clear communication, legal compliance, and partnerships with external resources are crucial elements of effective incident response. By continuously improving their incident response capabilities, organizations can enhance their overall cybersecurity resilience and minimize the impact of security incidents.

Chapter 9: Threat Deception and Active Defense

Deception technologies have emerged as a crucial component of active defense strategies in the ever-evolving field of cybersecurity. Next, we will explore the role and significance of deception technologies in enhancing an organization's ability to detect, respond to, and mitigate cyber threats.

At its core, deception technology is about creating a proactive defense mechanism that deceives, confuses, and misdirects potential attackers. It operates on the premise that adversaries will inevitably encounter decoy systems, data, or assets while attempting to infiltrate a network. Deception technologies leverage these decoys to detect and engage with malicious actors in real-time.

One of the key advantages of deception technologies is their ability to shift the balance of power away from attackers and towards defenders. Traditionally, security measures have been focused on building strong perimeter defenses, but determined attackers often find ways to breach these defenses. Deception technologies introduce a new layer of defense that actively engages with intruders once they are inside the network.

Deception techniques can be deployed across various layers of an organization's IT infrastructure, including endpoints, networks, and applications. Deceptive elements can take many forms, such as decoy servers, fake credentials, fabricated files, and counterfeit network traffic. These elements are designed to appear enticing to attackers while isolating them from genuine assets.

Deception technologies are highly dynamic and adaptable. They can mimic different types of systems, services, and behaviors to match an organization's specific environment. This adaptability allows organizations to create a convincing illusion that entices attackers to interact with the deceptive elements.

The deployment of deception technologies can serve multiple purposes. First and foremost, it provides early detection of intrusions. When an attacker interacts with a decoy system or credential, it triggers an alert, enabling security teams to respond promptly. This early detection can prevent attackers from moving laterally within the network and escalating their privileges.

Furthermore, deception technologies generate valuable threat intelligence. By analyzing how attackers interact with deceptive elements, organizations gain insights into their tactics, techniques, and procedures (TTPs). This intelligence can be used to refine security policies, improve incident response procedures, and enhance threat hunting efforts.

Deception technologies also introduce uncertainty for attackers. When intruders are unsure which assets are genuine and which are decoys, it becomes challenging for them to execute their attacks with confidence. This uncertainty can lead to hesitation, mistakes, and increased dwell time within the network, all of which benefit the defenders.

A notable aspect of deception technologies is their low false-positive rate. Because deception elements are rarely encountered by legitimate users or applications, alerts triggered by interactions with these elements are highly indicative of malicious activity. This reduces the noise that security teams must sift through, allowing them to focus on genuine threats.

Deception technologies support a proactive approach to threat mitigation. When an attacker is engaged with a decoy, security teams can gather real-time forensic data to understand the nature and scope of the attack. This information is invaluable for determining the appropriate response and mitigating the threat promptly.

In addition to real-time engagement, deception technologies facilitate threat deception. This involves manipulating an attacker's perception of the network environment to lead them away from valuable assets and into a labyrinth of decoys. By diverting attackers' attention and resources, organizations can buy time to respond effectively. The deployment of deception technologies is not a one-size-fits-all endeavor. Organizations must carefully consider their network architecture, assets, and the types of threats they are likely to face. Deception elements should be strategically placed to maximize their effectiveness while minimizing operational impact. Integration with existing security tools and processes is another crucial consideration. Deception technologies should complement and enhance an organization's existing security stack, including intrusion detection systems (IDS), security information and event management (SIEM) solutions, and incident response procedures. As with any security strategy, deception technologies require ongoing monitoring and maintenance. Deceptive elements must be regularly updated and refreshed to maintain their effectiveness. Security teams should also continuously analyze engagement data to refine their deception strategies.

Deception technologies are not a silver bullet for cybersecurity; they are most effective when used as part of a comprehensive security posture. They should be combined with other security measures, such as network segmentation, access controls, and regular security awareness training for employees.

In summary, deception technologies offer a proactive and dynamic approach to cybersecurity that empowers organizations to detect, engage with, and mitigate cyber threats in real-time. By leveraging the power of deception, organizations can shift the balance of power away from attackers and strengthen their overall security posture. As the threat landscape continues to evolve, deception technologies will play an increasingly critical role in defending against advanced adversaries.

Implementing active defense strategies is a critical component of modern cybersecurity practices. These strategies go beyond traditional passive measures and involve proactive engagement with potential threats to an organization's network and data. Active defense aims to disrupt, identify, and respond to malicious activities effectively. Next, we will explore the key principles and practical aspects of implementing active defense strategies in your cybersecurity program.

At its core, active defense is about taking the fight to cyber adversaries, making it more challenging for them to achieve their objectives. While passive defense strategies focus on hardening security perimeters and monitoring for breaches, active defense strategies involve actions that directly engage with attackers. These actions can range from luring attackers into controlled environments to actively disrupting their activities.

One fundamental concept in active defense is the use of deception techniques. Deception involves creating convincing lures, traps, and decoys within an organization's network or systems. These deceptive elements are designed to attract the attention of attackers and divert them from genuine assets. The goal is to make it difficult for adversaries to distinguish between real and fake assets, leading to confusion and mistakes on their part. Deception can take various forms, such as decoy servers, honey tokens, or fabricated files that mimic sensitive data. Deceptive credentials, misleading network traffic, and false endpoints are also commonly used. Deception technologies are highly adaptable and can mimic specific environments, applications, or services, making them appear authentic to attackers.

The deployment of deception elements should be strategic and well-planned. It's essential to consider an organization's unique network architecture and the likely attack vectors. Deception elements should be placed strategically to maximize their effectiveness while minimizing disruption to legitimate operations.

Another crucial aspect of active defense is threat intelligence integration. Organizations must have access to timely and relevant threat intelligence to inform their active defense strategies. Threat intelligence provides valuable insights into emerging threats, attacker tactics, and potential vulnerabilities. This information helps organizations prioritize their active defense efforts and refine their deception strategies.

One practical approach to active defense is the use of deception grids or networks. These networks consist of interconnected decoy systems and assets distributed across an organization's infrastructure. Attackers encountering these decoy elements are lured into the deception network, allowing security teams to monitor their activities closely. When attackers interact with deception elements, they trigger alerts that can lead to their identification and subsequent containment. Security teams can then gather valuable threat intelligence by analyzing how attackers engage with the deceptive assets. This intelligence informs incident response procedures and helps organizations better understand their adversaries' tactics, techniques, and procedures (TTPs).

Active defense is not solely reliant on deception technologies. It also involves active threat hunting, which is the proactive search for signs of malicious activity within an organization's network. Threat hunting often leverages threat intelligence and advanced analytics to identify potential threats that may have evaded automated detection mechanisms.

Furthermore, active defense strategies include taking countermeasures against attackers. This can involve disrupting their command and control infrastructure, diverting their attention, or impeding their lateral movement within the network. Countermeasures should be carefully planned to avoid unintended consequences or collateral damage.

Automation plays a significant role in active defense. Automated response mechanisms can be triggered based on predefined rules or threat intelligence feeds. These mechanisms can help organizations respond rapidly to detected threats and initiate actions to disrupt attacker activities.

While implementing active defense strategies, organizations should maintain a strong focus on incident response capabilities. Active engagement with attackers can lead to real-time incidents that require immediate attention. Having well-defined incident response procedures and a skilled incident response team is crucial to effectively mitigate threats.

Active defense should be integrated into an organization's overall cybersecurity strategy. It should complement existing security measures, including intrusion detection and prevention systems (IDS/IPS), firewalls, and security information and event management (SIEM) solutions. Coordination between active and passive defense measures ensures a holistic and robust security posture.

It's important to note that active defense should be conducted within the bounds of legal and ethical considerations. Organizations must adhere to laws and regulations governing cybersecurity practices. Engaging with attackers in a manner that may violate privacy or legal boundaries can have severe consequences.

In summary, implementing active defense strategies is a proactive approach to cybersecurity that empowers organizations to disrupt, identify, and respond to malicious activities effectively. Deception technologies, threat intelligence integration, threat hunting, and countermeasures all play vital roles in active defense. When integrated into a comprehensive cybersecurity program, active defense enhances an organization's ability to defend against evolving cyber threats. As the threat landscape continues to evolve, active defense will remain a critical component of a robust cybersecurity strategy.

Chapter 10: Security Metrics, Reporting, and Continuous Improvement

Key security metrics and Key Performance Indicators (KPIs) are essential tools for organizations to measure the effectiveness of their cybersecurity efforts. In today's rapidly evolving threat landscape, it's crucial to have a clear understanding of which metrics and KPIs matter most for monitoring and improving security posture. These metrics help organizations assess their vulnerabilities, detect and respond to threats, and make informed decisions to protect their digital assets.

One of the foundational security metrics is the number of security incidents detected and resolved over a specific period. This metric provides a high-level view of an organization's security posture and its ability to respond to threats promptly. A higher number of resolved incidents may indicate a proactive and effective security team.

Another important metric is the Mean Time to Detect (MTTD) and Mean Time to Respond (MTTR) to security incidents. MTTD measures the average time it takes to identify a security breach, while MTTR measures the average time it takes to contain and remediate the incident. Organizations aim to minimize both MTTD and MTTR to limit the potential impact of security incidents.

The number of vulnerabilities discovered and patched is a key metric for vulnerability management. This metric helps organizations assess their ability to identify and address security weaknesses in a timely manner. A high number of patched vulnerabilities indicates a proactive approach to risk mitigation.

The percentage of vulnerabilities that have been successfully patched or mitigated is another critical metric. A low percentage may indicate a backlog of unaddressed vulnerabilities that pose a significant risk to the organization.

A common metric for measuring the effectiveness of access control policies is the number of unauthorized access attempts or privilege escalation incidents. A higher number of unauthorized access attempts may indicate weaknesses in access control mechanisms or a growing threat from insider threats.

The ratio of false positives to true positives in security alerts is a crucial metric for evaluating the performance of intrusion detection and prevention systems (IDS/IPS) and other security technologies. A high ratio of false positives can lead to alert fatigue and a less effective security team.

The percentage of successful phishing simulations is a metric used to assess employee awareness and training programs. Organizations conduct phishing simulations to gauge their employees' ability to recognize and report phishing attempts. A lower success rate indicates that employees are becoming more security-conscious.

The number of open firewall ports or exposed services on external-facing systems is a metric used to evaluate an organization's attack surface. Reducing the number of open ports and services can help minimize the potential entry points for attackers.

The rate of security policy violations or non-compliance incidents is a key metric for ensuring that employees and systems adhere to security policies and regulations. A higher rate of policy violations may indicate the need for improved enforcement and user education.

The percentage of critical assets covered by comprehensive security monitoring and logging is a metric that reflects an organization's ability to detect and investigate security incidents. Comprehensive monitoring helps ensure that no critical assets are left unprotected.

The frequency and effectiveness of security training and awareness programs can be assessed by measuring the percentage of employees who complete training and demonstrate improved security behaviors. This metric helps organizations gauge the impact of their training efforts.

The percentage of security incidents that result in data breaches is a critical metric for understanding the impact of security incidents on sensitive data. Reducing this percentage is a top priority for organizations aiming to protect their valuable information.

The effectiveness of incident response plans can be measured by the time it takes to fully contain and remediate security incidents. Organizations strive to reduce this time to minimize the potential damage caused by incidents.

The financial impact of security incidents, including the cost of remediation, legal fees, and reputational damage, is a key metric for assessing the overall impact of cybersecurity incidents on the organization's bottom line. Reducing the financial impact of incidents is a primary goal for security teams.

In summary, key security metrics and KPIs are essential for organizations to assess their cybersecurity posture, measure the effectiveness of their security efforts, and make informed decisions to protect their digital assets. These metrics provide valuable insights into vulnerabilities, threat detection and response, access control, employee awareness, policy compliance, and incident impact. By monitoring and optimizing these metrics, organizations can enhance their overall security posture and adapt to the ever-changing threat landscape. Continuous improvement is a foundational principle in the world of security operations. In today's rapidly evolving threat landscape, organizations must constantly enhance their security operations to stay one step ahead of cyber adversaries. Achieving and maintaining a high level of security requires a commitment to ongoing improvement and adaptation. The process of continuous improvement involves regularly assessing and optimizing various aspects of security operations. This can encompass people, processes, technologies, and policies. One key aspect of continuous improvement is the refinement of incident response procedures.

As new threats emerge, incident response plans should be updated to address these evolving challenges.

Regularly testing and updating incident response plans ensures that security teams are well-prepared to handle a wide range of security incidents.

Another crucial element of continuous improvement is the enhancement of threat detection capabilities.

This involves deploying advanced technologies and techniques for identifying and mitigating emerging threats.

Machine learning and artificial intelligence are increasingly being used to bolster threat detection and response capabilities.

Additionally, organizations can benefit from threat intelligence feeds that provide real-time information about the latest cyber threats and vulnerabilities.

Regular training and development of security personnel are essential components of continuous improvement.

Security professionals must stay up-to-date with the latest cybersecurity trends and technologies.

This can be achieved through ongoing training programs, certifications, and participation in industry conferences and events.

The constant evolution of cyber threats necessitates a workforce that is knowledgeable and skilled in identifying and countering these threats.

Continuous improvement also extends to the monitoring and maintenance of security infrastructure.

Regularly updating security tools and software is critical for staying ahead of attackers who seek to exploit known vulnerabilities.

This includes not only patching and updating software but also regularly assessing the security configuration of systems and networks.

By conducting regular security assessments, organizations can identify and address weaknesses in their defenses.

Furthermore, organizations should regularly review and update their security policies and procedures.

This includes evaluating access control policies, data handling procedures, and compliance requirements.

Security policies should be adaptable to changing regulatory landscapes and emerging threats.

Collaboration and information sharing with industry peers play a vital role in continuous improvement.

By sharing insights and experiences, organizations can learn from one another's successes and failures.

Collaboration can lead to the development of best practices and innovative approaches to security challenges.

Regularly conducting penetration testing and vulnerability assessments is another essential aspect of continuous improvement.

These assessments help organizations identify and remediate weaknesses in their systems and networks before attackers can exploit them.

The results of these assessments can inform the organization's security strategy and help prioritize security investments.

Additionally, organizations can benefit from external assessments conducted by third-party experts.

These assessments provide an objective evaluation of an organization's security posture and recommendations for improvement.

Regularly reviewing and updating an organization's risk assessment is crucial for continuous improvement.

This involves identifying and prioritizing risks to the organization's assets and data.

By regularly reassessing risks, organizations can adjust their security strategies to address the most pressing threats.

The use of key performance indicators (KPIs) is essential for tracking progress in security operations.

KPIs can help organizations measure the effectiveness of their security efforts and identify areas in need of improvement.

Common KPIs include incident response times, the percentage of vulnerabilities remediated, and the frequency of security training.

Continuous improvement in security operations is not a one-time effort but an ongoing commitment.

It requires a proactive approach to identifying weaknesses and addressing them systematically.

The cybersecurity landscape is dynamic, with new threats constantly emerging.

To stay ahead of these threats, organizations must be agile and adaptable.

This means continuously evaluating and adjusting security strategies and investments.

Security leaders should regularly engage with executive leadership and the board of directors to communicate the importance of continuous improvement in security operations.

This includes providing updates on the evolving threat landscape and the organization's efforts to enhance security.

In summary, continuous improvement in security operations is a fundamental principle in today's cybersecurity landscape.

It involves regularly assessing and optimizing incident response procedures, threat detection capabilities, security personnel training, security infrastructure, policies and procedures, collaboration, penetration testing, risk assessments, and the use of KPIs.

By committing to continuous improvement, organizations can enhance their security posture and better protect their digital assets against evolving cyber threats.

Conclusion

In summary, the "Metasploit Masterclass for Ethical Hackers" book bundle offers a comprehensive and in-depth exploration of the world of ethical hacking, penetration testing, and vulnerability assessment. Across four meticulously crafted volumes, this bundle delves into the core facets of cybersecurity, equipping readers with the knowledge and skills needed to navigate the complex landscape of modern digital threats.

In Book 1, "Metasploit Masterclass: Network Reconnaissance and Vulnerability Scanning," readers embark on a journey through the foundational aspects of ethical hacking. They learn how to perform network reconnaissance, identify vulnerabilities, and conduct vulnerability scanning. This book serves as a solid starting point for those looking to build a strong ethical hacking skill set.

Moving on to Book 2, "Metasploit Masterclass: Web Application Penetration Testing," readers explore the intricacies of securing web applications. They discover how to identify and exploit vulnerabilities in web applications, gaining valuable insights into web security. This volume equips aspiring ethical hackers with the expertise needed to safeguard web-based systems effectively.

In Book 3, "Metasploit Masterclass: Wireless and IoT Hacking," the focus shifts to the rapidly evolving world of wireless networks and IoT devices. Readers learn how to exploit vulnerabilities in wireless networks, crack Wi-Fi passwords, and gain unauthorized access to IoT devices.

This book unveils the vulnerabilities of these technologies while providing valuable insights into securing them.

Finally, in Book 4, "Metasploit Masterclass: Advanced Threat Detection and Defense," readers dive into the realm of advanced threat detection and defense strategies. They explore proactive threat hunting, behavioral and anomaly-based detection, and the use of Metasploit for defensive purposes. This volume equips security professionals with the tools and techniques necessary to protect against sophisticated cyber threats.

Together, these four books create a cohesive and comprehensive resource for individuals aspiring to become ethical hackers or advance their cybersecurity careers. The "Metasploit Masterclass for Ethical Hackers" book bundle empowers readers to understand, identify, exploit, and defend against cyber threats, making it an invaluable addition to the library of any cybersecurity enthusiast or professional. Whether you are a novice looking to get started or an expert seeking to enhance your skills, this bundle provides the knowledge and expertise needed to excel in the dynamic and ever-evolving field of ethical hacking and cybersecurity.